Kursstufe Sek. II

Pathway Advanced

Abi *kompakt*

Thematic Vocabulary • Important Facts • Relevant Skills

Herausgegeben und erarbeitet von:
Iris Edelbrock

westermann GRUPPE

© 2017 Bildungshaus Schulbuchverlage
Westermann Schroedel Diesterweg Schöningh Winklers GmbH,
Georg-Westermann-Allee 66, 38104 Braunschweig
www.westermann.de

Das Werk und seine Teile sind urheberrechtlich geschützt.
Jede Nutzung in anderen als den gesetzlich zugelassenen bzw. vertraglich
zugestandenen Fällen bedarf der vorherigen schriftlichen Einwilligung des
Verlages. Nähere Informationen zur vertraglich gestatteten Anzahl von Kopien
finden Sie auf www.schulbuchkopie.de.

Für Verweise (Links) auf Internet-Adressen gilt folgender Haftungshinweis:
Trotz sorgfältiger inhaltlicher Kontrolle wird die Haftung für die Inhalte der
externen Seiten ausgeschlossen. Für den Inhalt dieser externen Seiten sind
ausschließlich deren Betreiber verantwortlich. Sollten Sie daher auf kosten-
pflichtige, illegale oder anstößige Inhalte treffen, so bedauern wir dies
ausdrücklich und bitten Sie, uns umgehend per E-Mail davon in Kenntnis
zu setzen, damit beim Nachdruck der Verweis gelöscht wird.

Druck A^3 / Jahr 2021
Alle Drucke der Serie A sind im Unterricht parallel verwendbar.

Redaktion: Marion Kramer
Umschlaggestaltung: Nora Krull, Bielefeld
Fotos: © John R. Rogers Photography (vorn) und stock.adobe.com/VladBrik (hinten)
Druck und Bindung:
Westermann Druck Zwickau GmbH, Crimmitschauer Straße 43, 08058 Zwickau

ISBN 978-3-14-**040184**-5

Contents

Focus on Vocab

Shaken, Not Stirred?! – The U.K. Between Tradition and Modernity   6
India: Democracy, Diversity and Determination   15
The American Dream – Reveries and Realities   21
The World Going Global: Opportunities and Options   34
Communication or Confusion? – English Around the World   47
Modern Media – Social, Smart and Spying?!   51

Focus on Facts

The British Empire   58
The Commonwealth of Nations   62
Great Britain – Immigration and Minorities   64
The European Union   68
The Political System of the United Kingdom   70
India: From Raj to Modern Democracy   72
American Beliefs and Values   76
The Civil Rights Movement: Fighting for Freedom and Equality   78
The United States: Immigration and Minorities   82
The Political System of the United States   84
The Colonization and Decolonization of Africa   88
Progress & Responsibility in a Global World   90
World Trade   92
The United Nations   94
Genetic Engineering   96
The Media   98

Focus on Skills

Basic Types of Fictional Texts 100
Basic Types of Non-Fictional Texts 102
Understanding Complex Texts 104
Analysis of a Fictional Text 106
Analysis of a Film Scene 108
Analysis of a Screenplay 110
Analysis of a Non-Fictional Text 112
Analysis of Poetry and Lyrics 114
Analysis of a Political Speech 116
Analysis of Statistical Data 118
Analysis of Visuals 120
Characterization of a Figure in Literature 124
Mediation 126
Conversation and Discussion 128
Oral Examinations 132
Giving a Speech 134
Presentations 136
Continuation of a Fictional Text 138
Writing a Comment and a Review 140
Writing an Analysis 142
Writing a Formal Letter 146
Writing an Interview 148
Writing a Newspaper Article 150
Writing a Speech Script 152
Writing a Summary 154
Writing a Letter to the Editor 156

Focus on Language

Connectives and Adverbs   158
Vocabulary and Phrases for Text Analysis   160

Thematic and Vocab Index   164
Picture acknowledgements   167

Note: This * sign indicates that the word/term can be found in the *Glossary of Literary Terms* in your Students' Book, pp. 405.

Shaken, Not Stirred?! – The U.K. Between Tradition and Modernity

English word/phrase	explanation in English	German equivalent and/or synonym(s)
the Commonwealth		
allegiance to sb./sth. [əˈliːdʒəns]	loyalty to a leader	*Loyalität/Ergebenheit gegenüber jmd.*
ceremonial position	a position that gives no real power	*zeremonielle/ förmliche Position*
declaration	an official statement	*(öffentliche) Erklärung, Bekanntgabe*
geopolitics	ideas and activities relating to the way that a country's position, population, etc. affect its political development and its relationship with other countries	*politische Geografie*
head of state	a leader or a person in charge of a state	*Staatsoberhaupt*
to share a common heritage	to have the same traditional beliefs, values, customs, etc.	*ein gemeinsames Erbe/Kultur haben*
intergovernmental	between different governments	*zwischenstaatlich, international*
legacy [ˈleɡəsi]	sth. that exists as a result of sth. that happened at an earlier time	*Erbe*
representative position	a position in which sb. represents a state, a community, an interest, etc.	*repräsentative Position*

self-determination	the right of the people to govern themselves	*Selbstbestimmung*
sovereign [ˈsɒvrɪn]; **sovereignty** [ˈsɒvrənti]	independent; complete freedom and power to govern	*uneingeschränkt, unabhängig, souverän; Eigenstaatlichkeit*

English word/phrase	explanation in English	German equivalent and/or synonym(s)
multicultural Britain		
alien	foreigner; foreign	*Fremder; fremd*
asylum seeker [əˈsaɪlem ˈsiːkə(r)]	sb. who leaves their own country because they are in danger and who asks the government of another country to allow them to live there	*Asylbewerber*
citizen; citizenship	a member of a state, subject; the legal right of belonging to a particular country	*Staatsbürger; Staatsbürgerschaft*
culture clash	a conflict arising from the interaction of people with different cultural values	*Zusammenprall der Kulturen*
(racial) discrimination	the practice of treating people in an unfair way because of their ethnicity	*(rassistische) Diskriminierung*
diversity [daɪˈvɜːsəti]	the fact of including many different types of people or things	*Vielfalt*
emigrant	sb. who leaves their own country to live in another	*Aussiedler, Emigrant*

to emigrate; emigration	to leave one's own country in order to live in another	*auswandern, emigrieren; Auswanderung, Emigration*
hospitable [hɒˈspɪtəbl]; **hospitality**	friendly and welcoming to visitors	*gastfreundlich; Gastfreundschaft*
identity crisis, crisis of identity	a feeling of uncertainty of who you really are and what your purpose is	*Identitätskrise*
immigrant	sb. who enters another country to live there permanently	*Einwanderer, Immigrant*
to immigrate; immigration	to come into a country in order to live there permanently	*einwandern, immigrieren; Einwanderung*
immigration control, border control	the place at an airport, sea port, etc. where officials check the documents of everyone entering the country	*Grenzkontrolle*
to integrate (sb. into/with); integration	to become part of a group or society and be accepted by them, or to help someone do this	*integrieren; Integration*
interracial marriage	marriage between people of different races	*Ehe zwischen Angehörigen verschiedener Ethnien*
labour shortage	a situation in which there are not enough workers	*Mangel an Arbeitskräften*
the middle class	the social class that includes people who are educated and work in professional jobs, e.g. teachers or managers	*die Mittelklasse/ Mittelschicht*

minority	a small group of people or things within a much larger group (= majority)	*Minderheit*
race relations	the relationship that exists between people from different countries, religions, etc. who are now living in the same place	*Beziehungen zwischen ethnischen Gruppen*
refugee [ˌrefjuˈdʒi]	sb. who has been forced to leave a country, esp. during a war, or for political or religious reasons	*Flüchtling*
temporary stay	a stay continuing for a limited period of time	*befristeter Aufenthalt*
Western values	the beliefs, traditions, customs, etc. of the Western community	*westliche Werte*

English word/phrase	explanation in English	German equivalent and/or synonym(s)
constitution/independence/treaties		
act	a law that has been officially accepted	*Gesetz*
bill	a written proposal for a new law that is brought to a parliament to be discussed	*Gesetzesentwurf*
charter/carta	a statement of the principles, duties and purposes of an organization	*Charta, Satzung*
constitutional document	an officially/legally accepted document	*Verfassungsurkunde*

constitutional monarchy, parliamentary monarchy	a country ruled by a king or queen whose power is limited by a constitution	konstitutionelle Monarchie
to deny sth. to sb., to deny sb. sth.	to refuse to allow sb. to have or do sth.	jdm. etwas verweigern/vorenthalten
despot ['despɒt]	tyrant ['taɪrənt]	Despot, Tyrann
Dominion	a country belonging to the British Empire or Commonwealth	Dominion (selbstständiges Land des Commonwealth)
to grant sb. sth., to grant sth. to sb.	to give sb. sth. or allow them to have sth. that they have asked for	jdm. etwas gewähren
to negotiate; negotiation	to discuss sth. in order to reach an agreement, esp. in business or politics	verhandeln; Verhandlung
petition	an official letter to a law court asking for a legal case to be considered	Petition, Antrag
referendum (on sth.)	when people vote to make a decision about a particular subject, rather than voting for a person	Referendum, Volksentscheid

English word/phrase	explanation in English	German equivalent and/or synonym(s)
British Empire		
diplomacy [dɪ'pləʊməsi]	the job or quality of managing the relationships between countries	Diplomatie, Verhandlungsgeschick
emperor/empress	the man/woman who rules an empire	Kaiser(in)

to expand; expansion	to become larger in size or number; growth	expandieren, sich vergrößern; Expansion, Wachstum
fall	loss of power, failure	Sturz, Umsturz
foreign policy	involving or dealing with other countries	Außenpolitik
to found sth.; foundation	to start sth., to establish sth.	etwas beginnen/ gründen; Gründung
to gain independence	to become independent	(an) Unabhängigkeit gewinnen
to grant sb. independence	to allow sb. to act on their own	jdm. Unabhängigkeit bewilligen
(policy of) imperialism	a political system in which one country rules a lot of other countries	Imperialismus; imperialistische Politik
indigenous [ɪnˈdɪdʒənəs]	native people who have always lived in a place	einheimisch
to be loyal to sb.	to support sb.	jdm. treu sein
maharaja [ˌmɑːhəˈrɑːdʒə]	an Indian prince or king	Maharadscha
overseas	to or in a foreign country that is across the sea	Übersee
to possess sth.	to own sth.	etwas besitzen
Raj [rɑːdʒ]	British rule in India	Britische Kolonialzeit in Indien
to reign	to rule a nation as their king, queen or emperor	regieren
rule	to have the official power to control a country	Herrschaft

self-government	a country or organization that is controlled by its own members	*Selbstverwaltung*
superiority over sth.	the quality of being better, more skilful, powerful, etc. than other people or things	*Überlegenheit*
viceroy [ˈvaɪsrɔɪ]	a man who was sent by a king or queen in the past to rule another country	*Vizekönig*

English word/phrase	explanation in English	German equivalent and/or synonym(s)
colonization		
the acquisition of colonies	here: the act of getting land	*Aneignung von Land/ Fläche*
to civilize sb.	to improve a society so that it is more organized and developed	*jdn. zivilisieren, jdm. Manieren beibringen*
to claim a territory	to conquer a territory	*ein Territorium erobern/in Anspruch nehmen*
colonial power	when a powerful country rules many weaker ones, and establishes its own trade and society there	*Kolonialmacht*
to colonize; colonization [ˌkɒləhnaɪˈzeɪʃn]	to establish political control over another country, and send your citizens there to settle	*kolonisieren, besiedeln; Kolonisierung, Besiedlung*

colony	a country/area that is under the political control of a more powerful country, usually one that is far away	*Kolonie*
colonist	sb. who settles in a new colony	*Kolonist, Siedler*
to conquer ['kɒŋkə(r)]; **conquest**	to take control of a country by fighting	*erobern; Eroberung, Sieg*
conqueror	a person (often an army) who fights to take control of a country	*Eroberer*
to decolonize sb.	to make a former colony politically independent	*jdn. entkolonialisieren/in die Unabhängigkeit entlassen*
to discover; discovery	if sb. discovers a new place, they are the first person to find it	*entdecken; Entdeckung*
to divide sth. up	to separate sth. into parts and share them between people	*etwas aufteilen*
to establish	to start e.g. an organization, esp. one that exists for a long time; to set up	*etwas gründen*
to exploit; exploitation	to try to get as much as you can out of a situation, sometimes unfairly	*ausnutzen, ausbeuten; Ausbeutung*
to explore; exploration	to travel to or around a place in order to learn about it	*erforschen; Erforschung, Erkundung*
to gain control over sb.	to obtain or achieve control over sb. you want or need	*Kontrolle über jdn. erlangen*

Focus on Vocab

to invade; invasion [ɪnˈveɪʒn]	to enter a country using military force in order to take control of it	einmarschieren; Einmarsch
mother country, motherland, fatherland	the country where someone was born (implies a strong emotional connection)	Herkunftsland, Vaterland
native	sb. who lives in a place all the time or has lived there a long time	Ureinwohner
negotiations	diplomatic talks to reach an agreement	Verhandlungen
postcolonial	later than or after colonialism	postkolonial
to settle; settlement	to go to a place where no people have lived permanently before and start to live there	(be-)siedeln; Besiedlung

India: Democracy, Diversity and Determination

English word/phrase	explanation in English	German equivalent and/or synonym(s)
historical development		
to gain independence (from)	to win political freedom from control by the government of another country	*Unabhängigkeit (von …) erlangen*
(historical) landmark	one of the most important events or discoveries	*wichtiges Datum*
to occupy; occupation of sth.	to enter a place and keep control of it (esp. by military force)	*belagern; Belagerung*
prehistory	time in history before everything was written down	*Prähistorie, Vorgeschichte*
to rebel [rɪˈbel]; **rebellion** [rɪˈbeljən]; **rebel** [ˈrebəl]	to oppose/fight against people in authority or against an idea which you do not agree with	*sich auflehnen, rebellieren; Rebellion, Widerstand; der Rebell*
to recapture sth. from sb.	to win back sth. that you already had in the past	*zurückerobern*
to revolt against sb./sth.; revolt [rɪˈvəʊlt]	to rebel; rebellion	*gegen etw./jdn. rebellieren; Aufstand*
tribe; tribal [ˈtraɪbl]	a social group whose members have the same customs, etc. and live in one particular area ruled by their leader; relating to a tribe or tribes	*(Volks-)Stamm; Stammes-*

English word/phrase	explanation in English	German equivalent and/or synonym(s)
challenges for a modern India		
caste [kɑːst] **system**	a hierarchical system of fixed social classes into which people are born	*Kastensystem, Kastenwesen*
challenge	sth. that tests strength, skill or ability	*Herausforderung*
to cope with	to succeed in dealing with a difficult problem	*mit etw. zurechtkommen*
crowded	too full of people or things	*überfüllt, beengt*
culture shock	the feeling of being confused or anxious that sb. gets when they visit a foreign country or a place very different from the one they are used to	*Kulturschock*
to face (a problem)	having to deal with a difficult situation	*vor einem Problem stehen*
foeticide [ˈfiːtɪˌsaɪd]	an act that causes the death of a (female) foetus	*absichtliches Töten eines (weiblichen) Fötus*
infrastructure	the basic systems and structures that a country needs in order to work properly, e. g. roads, railways, banks, hospitals, etc.	*(öffentliche) Einrichtungen, die für das Funktionieren einer Volkswirtschaft notwendig sind*
mobility	the ability to move easily from one job, area, or social class to another (also: social mobility)	*Mobilität, Bewegungsfreiheit, Freizügigkeit*

pollution	the process of making air, water, soil, etc. dangerously dirty and not suitable for people to use; the state of being dangerously dirty	*Verschmutzung*
population density	the degree to which an area is filled with people	*Bevölkerungsdichte*
to rape; rape	to force sb. to have sex	*vergewaltigen; Vergewaltigung*
rural	happening in or relating to the countryside	*ländlich, Land-*
sanitation	the protection of public health by removing and treating waste, dirty water, etc.	*Abwassersystem, Entsorgung; Hygiene*
slum	an area of a city that is in very bad condition, where very poor people live	*Elendsquartier, Armenviertel*
social inequality	an unfair situation in which some groups in society have more opportunities etc. than others	*soziale Ungleichheit*
(human) trafficking	the activity of taking people to another country and forcing them to work	*Menschenhandel*
traditional	following ideas and methods that have existed for a long time	*traditionell, althergebracht, überliefert*
urban growth	the expansion of cities	*Städtewachstum*

English word/phrase	explanation in English	German equivalent and/or synonym(s)
economy and trade		
to benefit from sth.; benefit	to get an advantage from sth.; advantage	*von etwas profitieren; Profit, Vorteil*
commerce [ˈkɒmɜːs]	trade	*Handel*
corruption	dishonest, illegal or immoral behaviour, esp. from sb. in power, often involving money	*Korruption, Bestechung*
demand	the need or desire people have for particular goods and services	*Nachfrage*
developing country	a poor country that is trying to increase its industry and trade and improve life for its people	*Entwicklungsland*
(the) digital age	a period in history that is characterized by the shift from traditional industry to an economy based on information technology	*das digitale Zeitalter, Computer-, Internet-Zeitalter*
economic growth	relating to a positive development of a country's economy	*Wirtschaftswachstum*
economic power	a country that is economically strong and important and can influence events	*Wirtschaftskraft, Wirtschaftsmacht*
economy	the system by which a country's money and goods are produced and used, or a country considered in this way	*Wirtschaft*

emerging market	a country/an economy in an early stage of development, a country that does not (yet) meet the standards of a developed market	*Schwellenland, Wachstumsmarkt*
to export sth. [ɪkˈspɔːt]; **export**	to sell goods to another country	*etw. exportieren; Warenexport, Warenausfuhr*
foreign investment	business and investments of money involving other countries	*Auslandsinvestitionen*
goods (*pl.*)	things that are produced in order to be sold	*Waren*
living standard	the level of comfort and the amount of money people have; standard of living	*Lebensstandard*
low-wage country	a country where workers only earn very little money	*Niedriglohnland*
to import sth.; import of goods	to bring a product from one country into another so that it can be sold there	*etw. importieren; Warenimport, Wareneinfuhr*
to manufacture sth.; manufacturing	to produce sth.; the process or business of producing goods in factories; production	*etw. herstellen; Produktion, Fertigung*
(natural) resources [rɪˈsɔːsəz]	soil, minerals, forests, water and energy sources	*natürliche Ressourcen*

Focus on Vocab

outsourcing	when a company uses workers from outside the company to do a job	*Ausgliederung von Produktion oder Dienstleistungen an Externe*
to provide sth.	to make sth. available	*zur Verfügung stellen*
raw [rɔ:] materials	natural substances that are used in manufacturing goods	*Rohstoffe*
supply and demand	the relationship between the quantity of goods for sale and the quantity of goods that people want to buy, esp. the way it influences prices	*Angebot und Nachfrage*
sweatshop	a small business, factory, etc. where people work hard in bad conditions for very little money	*ausbeuterischer Betrieb*
to trade	to buy and sell goods	*handeln; Handel treiben*
trade route [treɪd ruːt]	a way across land or sea used by traders	*Handelsweg*
trading company	business that buys and sells goods, esp. internationally	*Handelsgesellschaft*
waste imports	litter/rubbish that is brought from one country to another so that it can be sold to businesses that specialize in treating, dumping or burning it	*Einfuhr von Abfällen*

The American Dream – Reveries and Realities

English word/phrase	explanation in English	German equivalent and/or synonym(s)
US history		
to abolish sth. [əˈbɒlɪʃ]; **abolition of sth.** [ˌæbəˈlɪʃn]	to officially end a law, a system	*etwas abschaffen; Abschaffung*
to become independent of sb./sth.	to be one's own master	*von jdm./etw. unabhängig werden*
independence	freedom from political control by the government of another country	*Unabhängigkeit*
civil rights movement	citizens who fight for the rights that each person has in a society, whatever their race, sex or religion	*Bürgerrechtsbewegung*
discrimination	the practice of treating a person or group less fairly than others	*Diskriminierung*
to escape persecution	to get away from persecution	*Verfolgung entgehen; fliehen*
to found sth.	to start sth., e.g. an organization, a company, etc.	*etwas gründen*
Founding Fathers	sb. who begins sth., e.g. a new way of thinking (here: Thomas Jefferson, Benjamin Franklin, George Washington, etc.)	*Gründungsväter*

Focus on Vocab

the Frontier ['frʌntɪə(r)]	the border between settled/civilized and unsettled/uncivilized country	*das Grenzland*
to gain independence	to become independent	*Unabhängigkeit erlangen*
interventionism	the policy of intervening in the affairs of another sovereign state	*Interventionismus*
isolationism	the policy of nonparticipation in international economic and political relations	*Isolation, Isolationismus*
native	a word used by white people to refer to the people who lived in America, etc. before Europeans arrived	*Ureinwohner*
pilgrim	a religious person who travels to a holy place	*Pilger*
plantation	a large piece of land where crops are grown	*Plantage*
prejudice ['predʒudɪs]	an unreasonable dislike of people who are different	*Vorurteil*
to be prejudiced	having an unreasonable dislike of sb. or sth., mostly because of foreignness	*voreingenommen sein, Vorurteile haben*
protest movement	a large group of people who come together to publicly express disapproval or opposition to sth.	*Protestbewegung*

purchase [ˈpɜːtʃəs]	sth. you buy	*Ankauf*
Puritan [ˈpjʊərɪtən]	a member of a Protestant religious sect in the 16th and 17th centuries, who wanted to make religion simpler	*Puritaner(in)*
racial segregation	when people of different races are kept apart so that they live, work or study separately	*Rassentrennung*
to rebel [rɪˈbel]; **rebellion** [rɪˈbeljən]	to oppose or fight against people in authority or against an idea or a situation which you do not agree with; an organized attempt to change the government or a leader of a country, using violence	*rebellieren; Rebellion, Aufstand*
subject (*fml.*)	here: citizen	*Staatsbürger*
trading post	a place where people can buy and exchange goods far away from town, esp. in the past	*Handelsstützpunkt*

English word/phrase	explanation in English	German equivalent and/or synonym(s)
politics/constitution		
administration	the government of a country	*Regierung, Verwaltung*
amendment	a change to a law that is still being discussed	*Zusatz (zur Verfassung)*
to amend [əˈmend] **a bill**	to make changes to a (draft) law	*eine Gesetzesvorlage/ ein Gesetz ändern*

Focus on Vocab

appointment	the act of choosing sb. for a position or job	Ernennung
article	paragraph (of a law)	Paragraf, Artikel
civil servant	sb. employed in the civil service	Beamter
Constitution	a set of basic laws and principles that a country or organization is governed by	Verfassung
to declare sth. unconstitutional	to say officially that sth. is not allowed by the constitution	etwas für verfassungswidrig erklären
domestic policy	the internal policy of a country without involving other countries	Innenpolitik
to ensure (a right)	to make certain that sth. will happen properly; to assure	zusichern
foreign policy	involving or dealing with other countries	Außenpolitik
to govern	to rule	regieren
grass roots (democracy)	the ordinary people rather than the rulers	Basis, „Fußvolk"
Head of State	the main representative of a country, e.g. a king	Staatsoberhaupt
to interfere with sth.	to prevent sth. from happening the way that it was planned	sich in etwas einmischen
policy	a set of ideas of what to do in certain situations that has been agreed on by a government or a party	eine bestimmte Politik

politician [ˌpɒləˈtɪʃn]	sb. who works in politics, esp. an elected member of the government	*Politiker*
political [pəˈlɪtɪkl]	relating to governmental actions or people	*politisch*
to be (politically) impartial	not supporting one person or group more than another	*unparteiisch sein*
to ratify a treaty	to make a treaty official by signing it	*einen Vertrag unterzeichnen*
reunification	to join the parts of sth. together again, esp. a country that was divided	*Wiedervereinigung*

English word/phrase	explanation in English	German equivalent and/or synonym(s)
beliefs/values		
achievement	sth. that you succeed in doing by your own efforts	*Errungenschaft*
authority [ɔːˈθɒrəti]	the power you have because of your official position	*Autorität, Amtsgewalt*
cultural patterns/ habits	cultural ideas/ behaviour	*kulturelle Gewohnheiten*
divine providence	what is thought to be God's intervention in the world	*göttliche Vorsehung*
to be equal; equality [iˈkwɒləti]	to have the same rights and opportunities as everyone else, no matter what your sex, race, age, religion, etc.	*gleichgestellt sein; Gleichheit, Gleichberechtigung*

God's chosen people	in 1630, the founding Puritans believed they were the chosen people of God and had the duty to build an ideal Christian community in the new World	*Gottes auserwähltes Volk*
heterogeneous society [ˌhetərəˈdʒiːniəs]	a very diverse society	*verschiedenartige, breit gefächerte Gesellschaft*
to identify with sb./sth.; identification [aɪˌdentɪfɪˈkeɪʃn]	to feel sympathy for sb./sth. or be able to share their feelings; a strong feeling of sympathy and similarity with sb.	*sich mit jdm./etw. identifizieren; Identifikation*
inalienable/ unalienable rights [ɪnˈeɪliənəbl]	rights that cannot be taken from you	*unveräußerliche Rechte*
individuality [ˌɪndɪˌvɪdʒuˈæləti]	the qualities that make sb. or sth. different from other people or things	*Individualität*
Manifest Destiny [ˈmænɪfest ˈdestəni]	the belief that the US people had the right and the duty to take land in North America from other people, because this was God's plan	*offensichtliche Bestimmung (amerik. Doktrin des 19. Jahrhunderts; göttlicher Auftrag zur Expansion)*
Melting Pot	the idea of a place where people's different races, cultures, etc. blend together into one nation	*Schmelztiegel (der Kulturen)*
national anthem	the official song of a nation	*Nationalhymne*

national pride	being proud of having a particular nationality	Nationalstolz
to offer an opportunity to sb.	to give sb. a chance to do sth.	eine Gelegenheit bieten
patriotism [ˈpeɪtriətɪzəm]	when you love your country and are proud of it; national pride	Patriotismus
(to be) patriotic	having or expressing a great love of your country	patriotisch (sein)
prosperity	wealth	Reichtum, Wohlstand
Pursuit of Happiness [pəˈsjuːt]	the act of trying to find happiness	Streben nach Glück, existenzieller Sicherheit, Zufriedenheit
rags-to-riches	the idea of becoming very rich after starting life very poor	vom Tellerwäscher zum Millionär
religious tolerance [rɪˈlɪdʒəs ˈtɒlərəns]	not discriminating against people from different religions	religiöse Toleranz
self-improvement	the process of trying to become a better person	(selbstständige) Weiterbildung
thrift	the habit of saving money and spending it carefully	Wirtschaftlichkeit, Sparsamkeit
unlimited possibilities	endless/limitless opportunities and possibilities	unbegrenzte Möglichkeiten

English word/phrase	explanation in English	German equivalent and/or synonym(s)
immigration/minorities		
alien	a person who is not a citizen of the country in which they live and work	*Fremde/r*
to assimilate; assimilation	to become a part of a country/community	*anpassen/Anpassung*
border control	measures taken to prevent illegal immigrants from entering a country; immigration control	*Grenzkontrolle*
citizen	a person who has the legal right to belong to a particular country	*Staatsbürger*
descendant	sb. who is related to a person that lived a long time ago	*Nachkomme*
to emigrate (from); emigration	to leave one's own country in order to live in another	*auswandern; Auswanderung*
ethnic; ethnicity	connected with a nation, race or people that shares certain cultural traditions	*ethnisch; Ethnizität, Volkszugehörigkeit*
illegal alien	an illegal immigrant	*illegaler Einwanderer*
Hispanic	a person whose first language is Spanish, esp. one who comes from a Latin American country	*Lateinamerikaner(in), Südamerikaner(in)*
to immigrate (to) ['ɪmɪgreɪt]	to come into a country in order to live there	*immigrieren, einwandern*

immigration control	the place where the passports and other documents of people coming into the country are checked	*Einwanderungskontrolle*
(cultural) interaction	the act of communicating with sb. (from a different culture)	*(kulturelle) Interaktion*
multi-ethnic	involving or including different ethnicities	*Vielvölker-*
naturalization	to become a citizen of a particular country	*Einbürgerung*
to be processed through sth.	to be moved forward from one checkpoint to the next	*durchgereicht werden, weitergeschickt werden*
to take an oath of allegiance	a formal promise to be loyal to a country	*den Treueeid schwören*

English word/phrase	explanation in English	German equivalent and/or synonym(s)
economy		
to go bankrupt; bankruptcy	to become officially unable to pay your debts; to go bust; the state of being unable to pay your debts	*Pleite gehen; Pleite, Bankrott*
capitalism [ˈkæpɪtəlɪzəm]	an economic and political system in which businesses belong mostly to private owners, not to the government	*Kapitalismus*
capitalist [ˈkæpɪtəlɪst]	sb. who owns or controls a lot of money and lends it to businesses, banks, etc. to produce more wealth	*Kapitalist*

commerce	trade	*Handel*
to drop; drop	to fall to a lower level or amount; reduction	*fallen, einbrechen; Absturz, Abfall*
financial recession	a difficult time when there is less business activity, trade, etc. in a country	*finanzielle Rezession, Flaute*
hire and fire policy	to employ and dismiss people in quick succession	*Einstellen und Feuern von Beschäftigten*
homeowner(s)	people who own their home	*Hauseigentümer*
to be low-income	to be below an acceptable or usual level of income	*geringverdienend sein*
ownership society	a society in which personal responsibility, economic liberty, and the possession of property are very important	*von G. W. Bush vertretenes Gesellschaftsmodell, in dem die Bürger für sich und ihr Wohlergehen zuständig sind*
real estate ['riːəl ɪ'steɪt] (*US*)	property in the form of land and houses	*Grundbesitz*
to regenerate [rɪ'dʒenəreɪt]	to make sth. develop and grow strong again	*erneuern, umgestalten*
to subsidize ['sʌbsɪdaɪz]	if a government subsidizes a company, activity, etc., it pays parts of its costs	*subventionieren*
subsidy ['sʌbsədi]	money that is paid by a government or organization to make prices lower and reduce the cost of producing goods	*Subvention*

to tax sb.	to pay an amount of money to the government according to your income, property, etc.	*jdn./etwas besteuern*
tax system	the system of charging taxes	*Steuersystem*
upward mobility	the act of moving up through the social classes and becoming richer	*sozialer Aufstieg*
to be wealthy; wealth [welθ]	to have a lot of property, money, etc.; a large amount of money, etc. that sb. owns	*wohlhabend sein; Wohlstand*

English word/phrase	explanation in English	German equivalent and/or synonym(s)
crises/war/poverty		
to accomplish a mission	to succeed in doing sth.	*eine Mission erfüllen*
combat	fighting, esp. during a war	*Kampf, Gefecht*
civil war	a war in which opposing groups of people from the same country fight each other to gain political control	*Bürgerkrieg*
crisis (crises) ['kraɪsɪs]	situation(s) in which problems must be dealt with quickly	*Krise (Krisen)*
to declare war on sb.	to start a war against someone	*jdm. den Krieg erklären*
the (Great) Depression	the world economic crisis during the 1930s	*Weltwirtschaftskrise*

to fall into poverty	to become poor	*verarmen, in Armut stürzen*
to invade; invasion of a country	to enter a country using military force in order to control it	*eindringen, überfallen; Überfall, Einmarsch in ein Land*
occupant	member of the occupying force	*Besatzer*
to occupy ['ɒkjupaɪ]; **occupation of** [ˌɒkjuˈpeɪʃn]	to enter a place in a large group and keep control of it, esp. by military force	*belagern, besetzen; Besatzung*
pre-military training	training that people get before joining the army	*militärische Vorbereitung, Training*
to recruit sb. [rɪˈkruːt]	to hire sb.	*jdn. rekrutieren/ einstellen*
retaliation	an action against sb. who has done sth. bad to you	*Vergeltung*
social benefits	money provided by the government to people who are not able to work	*Sozialhilfe*
social ranking	related to the social classes people belong to	*soziale Rangordnung*
tense (*adj.*); **tension**	feeling worried, uncomfortable and unable to relax; the feeling that exists when people or countries do not trust each other and may suddenly attack each other	*(an)gespannt; Spannung*

welfare (state)	a system in which the government provides money, medical care, etc. for people who are unemployed or not able to work	*Wohlfahrtsstaat*
to withdraw; withdrawal	to stop taking part in an activity; to move away an army from the area where they were fighting	*sich zurückziehen; Rückzug*

The World Going Global: Opportunities and Options

English word/phrase	explanation in English	German equivalent and/or synonym(s)
trade		
(economic) supremacy [suːˈpreməsi]	the position in which a country/an economy is more powerful or advanced than others	*Übermacht, Überlegenheit*
industrialized country	a country that has a lot of factories, etc.	*Industrieland*
Industrial Revolution	the period in the 18th and 19th centuries in Europe and the US when machines began to be used to do work, and industry grew rapidly	*Industrielle Revolution*
secure markets	safe markets	*sichere Märkte*
shipping	the delivery of goods	*Lieferung, Zustellung*
trade embargo	trade boycott	*Handelsembargo, -sperre*
taxation	the system of charging taxes	*Besteuerung*

English word/phrase	explanation in English	German equivalent and/or synonym(s)
consumerism and consumption		
acquisition of sth.	the act of buying sth.	*Anschaffung, Erwerb*
availability [əˌveɪləˈbɪlɪti]	the fact that sb. is free to be contacted; the fact that sth. is there to be bought	*Verfügbarkeit*
consumer	sb. who buys and uses products and services	*Konsument*

customer	sb. who buys goods or services from a shop, company, etc.	*Kunde*
discount shopping	to go shopping at a store that sells goods cheaply	*Kauf von preisreduzierter Ware*
distribution of sth.	the act of giving or delivering sth. to a number of people	*Verteilung*
efficiency [ɪˈfɪʃənsi]	the quality of doing sth. well without wasting money or time	*Effizienz, Effektivität*
industrialized mass production	when products are made in large numbers by industrial machines so they can be sold cheaply	*industrielle Massenproduktion*
to instil a desire	to put the idea in sb.'s mind that they desire sth.	*in jdm. eine Begierde wecken*
Internet retailer	Internet shop	*Internet-Versandhandel*
to line the shelves	to offer sth. for sale in large amounts	*den Absatz steigern*
mounting consumer debt	strongly rising consumer debt	*steigende Konsumentenverschuldung*
online shopping portal	a website where you can buy things	*Plattform für Online-Einkäufe*
purchasing power	the amount of money a person or group has available to spend	*Kaufkraft*
range of products	selection of products	*Produktauswahl, Produktpalette*
retailer/retail store	a person or store that sells goods	*Händler, Einzelhändler*

Focus on Vocab

English word/phrase	explanation in English	German equivalent and/or synonym(s)
trade unions and labour policy		
company board	a group of elected or appointed members who supervise the activities of a company	*Aufsichtsrat*
company pension plan	an arrangement between a company and its employees (or a union representing the employees) to provide money (a retirement pension) for the employees' retirement	*betriebliche Altersvorsorge*
to dismiss	to officially remove sb. from their job	*jdn. entlassen*
employment legislation	laws that govern the employer-employee relations and rights of employees; labour legislation	*Arbeitsrecht*
freelancing	working independently (for different companies)	*freiberuflich arbeiten*
(to work) flexitime	system in which employees work a particular number of hours each week/month but can choose when they start and finish work	*flexible Arbeitszeiten*
(to work) full-time	for all the hours of a week/month which people normally work	*Vollzeit-*

labour contract	contract between employee and employer	*Arbeitsvertrag*
labour market	the number of people who are available for work in relation to the number of jobs available	*Arbeitsmarkt*
to lay off (laid off, laid off)	to stop employing sb.	*entlassen*
(to work) overtime	working more hours than you have to according to your contract	*Überstunden, Mehrarbeit*
(to work) part-time	working for part of the day/week	*Teilzeit-, in Teilzeit*
paternity/maternity leave	time that a father/mother is allowed to spend away from work when they have a baby	*Erziehungsurlaub*
personnel [ˌpɜːsənˈel]	the people working in a firm, etc.; staff	*Personal*
salary	wage, pay; money that you receive for doing your job	*(Jahres-/Monats-) Gehalt*
to (go on) strike	to refuse to work in order to protest against sth.	*streiken*
unemployment benefit	money paid by the government to sb. who is unemployed	*Arbeitslosengeld*
(trade) union	organization of workers to protect their interests	*Gewerkschaft*
wages (*pl.*)	pay, salary; money that you receive for doing your job	*Lohn, Löhne*

| works council | a group representing the employees of a company whose members are elected to negotiate working conditions, etc. with the company's management | *Betriebsrat* |

English word/phrase	explanation in English	German equivalent and/or synonym(s)
globalisation		
capital market	financial market	*Finanzmarkt, Kapitalmarkt*
cultural imperialism	the imposing of a foreign culture on sb.	*kultureller Imperialismus*
domestic demand	amount of money spent on goods and services by the people, companies and government within a particular country	*inländische Nachfrage*
domestic labour market	the number of workers and available jobs within a particular country	*inländischer Arbeitsmarkt*
entrepreneurship [ˌɒntrəprə'nɜːʃɪp]	running one's own business	*Unternehmertum*
expatriate	a person living (and working) in a country that is not their own	*jmd., der sein Heimatland verlässt, um Arbeit zu finden*
to generate capital	to yield/produce money	*Kapital erwirtschaften*
global labour market	global workforce	*globaler Arbeitsmarkt*

infrastructure	the basic systems and services, such as transport or power supplies, that a country or organization uses in order to work effectively	*Infrastruktur*
interdependency	a situation in which people or things depend on each other	*Korrelation, gegenseitige Abhängigkeit*
to internationalize	to make sth. become international	*etw. internationalisieren*
labour standards	the working conditions	*Arbeitsgesetzgebung*
liberalization of sth.	the act of making sth. less strict	*Liberalisierung von etw.*
logistics	the practical organization of sth.	*Logistik*
migrant worker	sb. who moves to a richer country in order to work there	*Wanderarbeiter, Gastarbeiter*
multinationals	large companies that operate in several countries	*multinationale Konzerne*
output	amount of sth. that a company produces	*Produktion, Leistung*
outsourcing of work	the act of arranging for sb. outside the company to do work for that company	*Ausgliederung/ Auslagerung von Arbeit*
to promote international trade	to do sth. in order to increase international trade	*internationalen Handel fördern*
protectionism	when a government tries to help industries in its own country by taxing or restricting goods	*Protektionismus, Schutzpolitik*

to raise living standards	to improve the level of comfort and increase the amount of money that people have	*Lebensstandards erhöhen*
repatriate	a person who has lived and worked abroad and returns to his or her homeland	*jmd., der in sein Heimatland zurückkehrt*
trade negotiation [nɪˌgəʊʃiˈeɪʃn]	discussion in order to reach an agreement on trade	*Wirtschaftsverhandlung(en)*
unskilled worker	sb. who works in a job that requires little or no training	*Hilfskraft, ungelernter Arbeiter*

English word/phrase	explanation in English	German equivalent and/or synonym(s)
ecology and energy		
carbon emission	carbon dioxide that planes, cars, factories, etc. produce, which is harmful to the environment	*Kohlenstoffausstoß*
climate change	a permanent change in weather conditions	*Klimawandel*
crops	plants that are grown by farmers and used as food	*Getreide*
deforestation	the cutting or burning down of all the trees in an area	*Waldrodung*
exploitation	when sb. treats sb. else unfairly – esp. to make money from their work	*Ausbeutung*

fracking (hydraulic fracturing)	a technique used to force oil and natural gas from rock by pumping pressurized fluid into the ground and creating new channels in the rock which makes oil, etc. more easily available	*Fracking*
fragility of sth.	the quality of being easily broken or damaged	*Zerbrechlichkeit*
fossil fuel	fuel such as coal and oil, which were formed underground from plant and animal remains millions of years ago	*fossiler Brennstoff*
greenhouse effect	the gradual warming of the air surrounding the earth as a result of heat being trapped by pollution	*Treibhauseffekt*
to have an impact on sth.	to influence sth.	*etw. beeinflussen*
heatwave	a period of unusually hot weather	*Hitzewelle*
the incineration of trash	the act of burning trash in a facility	*Müllverbrennung*
to pose a threat for/ to sb.	to create a threat, problem, etc. that has to be dealt with	*für jdn. eine Bedrohung darstellen*
renewable energies	types of energy such as wind or solar power that can be replaced as quickly as they are used	*erneuerbare Energien*

sustainability [sə͵steɪnəˈbɪlɪti]	able to continue for a long time without causing damage to the environment	*Nachhaltigkeit*
waste disposal	getting rid of garbage	*Müllentsorgung*
water supply	the water that is provided and treated for a particular area	*Wasserversorgung*

English word/phrase	explanation in English	German equivalent and/or synonym(s)
democracy		
amendment [əˈmendmənt]	an addition to a law or document	*Ergänzung, Gesetzesnovelle*
to cast one's ballot/ vote	to vote in an election	*eine Stimme abgeben*
collective military action	military action that is carried out by more than one country, member state, etc.	*gemeinsame militärische Aktion*
to declare sth. unconstitutional	to declare that a law or rule is not allowed by the constitution of a country or organization	*etw. für nicht verfassungsgemäß erklären*
diplomacy [dɪˈpləʊməsi]	the job or activity of managing the relationships between countries	*Diplomatie*
electorate	the people in a country who have the right to vote	*Wähler, Wählerschaft*
General Assembly	representatives of all the member nations of the United Nations	*Vollversammlung*

to impose sanctions	to use official orders or laws as a way of forcing a leader of another country to make political changes	*Sanktionen verhängen*
inaugural address	the first speech of a new leader	*Amtsantrittsrede*
inauguration	the ceremony of putting sb. into an official position	*Amtseinführung*
legislation	a law or a set of laws	*Gesetzgebung*
to maintain peace	to make peace continue	*Frieden aufrechterhalten*
to mediate between	to try to end a disagreement between two or more people or groups by talking to them	*vermitteln (zwischen)*
oath of office	a formal promise sb. takes before undertaking the duties of an office	*Amtseid*
to run for president	to be a candidate in an election for president	*als Präsident(in) kandidieren*
separation of powers	the principle of dividing the political power of a government into an executive, a legislative and a judicial branch	*Gewaltentrennung*
to serve a term	to spend a fixed or limited period of time in a job	*eine Amtszeit lang dienen*

system of checks and balances	the principle of government (in the US) by which the President, Congress and the Supreme Court each have some control over the others	*Gewaltenteilung (gegenseitige Kontrolle der drei Gewalten)*
tribunal [traɪˈbjuːnl]	a type of court that is given official authority	*Tribunal, Gericht*

English word/phrase	explanation in English	German equivalent and/or synonym(s)
political systems		
administration	the government of a country at a particular time	*Regierung*
to amend (a bill) [əˈmend]; **amendment**	to correct or make changes to sth.; an addition to a law or document	*(ein Gesetz) ändern, ergänzen; Gesetzesänderung; Zusatzartikel*
to dissolve (parliament)	to officially end (parliament)	*auflösen*
domestic policy	laws and policies that apply within a particular nation's borders	*Innenpolitik*
to be eligible to vote	to be legally allowed to vote	*wahlberechtigt sein*
first-past-the-post system	a voting system in which the person who gets the most votes is elected; majority vote	*Mehrheitswahlrecht*
foreign policy	policy dealing with or involving other countries	*Außenpolitik*

proportional representation	a political system in which parties are represented in parliament according to the number of votes	*Verhältniswahlrecht*
universal suffrage [ˈsʌfrɪdʒ]	the right of all the people in the country to vote	*allgemeines Wahlrecht*

English word/phrase	explanation in English	German equivalent and/or synonym(s)
science and technology		
artificial intelligence	the study of how to make computers copy intelligent human behaviour	*künstliche Intelligenz*
assembly line production	a system of making things in which the product moves past a line of workers who each make or check one part	*Fließbandproduktion*
to develop sth.	to think of or produce a new product; to design	*entwickeln*
drone	a vehicle, e.g. an aircraft or missile, that does not have a pilot but is remote-controlled	*unbemanntes (Luft-)Fahrzeug*
enhanced [ɪnˈhɑːnst]	improved, better	*erweitert, verbessert*
findings	results	*Ergebnisse*
to invent sth.; invention	to make, design or think of a new type of thing; a useful machine, tool, instrument, etc. that has been invented	*etw. erfinden; Erfindung*

microelectronics [ˌmaɪkrəʊˌɪlek'trɒnɪks]	the science and technology involved in the making and using of very small electronic parts	*Mikroelektronik*
progress; progressive	the process of improving or developing, or of getting closer to finishing or achieving sth.; in favour of new or modern ideas, methods and change	*Fortschritt; fortschrittlich*
research; researcher	the careful study of a subject; sb. who studies a subject in detail in order to discover new information	*Forschung, Recherche; Forscher*
to verify	to determine whether sth. is correct, to confirm	*überprüfen, bestätigen*

Communication or Confusion? – English Around the World

English word/phrase	explanation in English	German equivalent and/or synonym(s)
language		
accent [ˈæksənt]	manner of pronunciation characteristic of a region	*Akzent*
acronym	a word formed from the first letters of the words that make up the name of sth., e.g. UN (United Nations)	*Akronym, Kurzwort*
antonym	a word that is opposite in meaning to another word	*Gegensatzwort*
bilingual [baˈlɪŋgwəl]	a person with a command of two languages	*zweisprachig*
colloquial; colloquialism	used in conversation but not in formal speech or writing; an informal expression or word	*umgangssprachlich; umgangssprachlicher Ausdruck*
communication	activity of exchanging information or meaning	*Kommunikation, Austausch*
communicative competence	a person's awareness of the rules governing the appropriate use of language in social situations	*kommunikative Fähigkeit/Kompetenz*

Focus on Vocab

communication strategies	strategies of expressing meaning (e.g. in a second language) without knowing the exact words for it	*kommunikative Strategien*
dialect	variety of language common among a group of speakers, usually defined by region	*Dialekt, lokale/ regionale Sprach- variante*
ESL [ˌiːesˈel]	English as a Second Language	*Englisch als Zweit- sprache*
four-letter words	swear/curse words	*Schimpfwort, Kraftausdruck*
Globish (Global English)	a simplified form of international English	*internationales Englisch*
idiom	combination of words in common use; an expression that cannot be translated word for word	*Redensart*
lingua franca	a medium of communication used by people who speak different first languages	*Verkehrssprache, Lingua franca*
literary freedom	personal variation of language as used by writers, poets, etc.	*dichterische Freiheit*
loanword/borrowing	a word from another language used in its original form	*Lehnwort*
mother tongue	the language that you first learn to speak as a child	*Muttersprache*

multilingual	a person with a command of several languages	*mehrsprachig*
native speaker	a speaker of a certain language as a first language	*Muttersprachler*
Netspeak	language used to communicate on the Internet	*Netzjargon*
non-Standard English	informal or slang vocabulary, grammar or pronunciation	*umgangssprachliches Englisch*
paraphrase	an alternate way of saying sth.	*Umschreibung*
phrase	a group of words that together have a particular meaning	*Wendung*
primary language	the language you learned first, or the one you use most often	*Primärsprache*
pronunciation	the way in which a word is spoken	*Aussprache*
Queen's English (*outdated*)	the standard accent of British English; sometimes also called Oxford English	*Standardenglisch, britisches Englisch*
register	language used in a particular social environment	*Sprachebene*
secondary language	a person's second language or one that is used less often	*Zweitsprache*
slang	informal, non-standard vocabulary	*Umgangssprache*

sociolect	variety of language common among the members of a specific social group	*Soziolekt, Gruppensprache*
synonym	a word that has the same meaning as another word	*sinnverwandtes Wort*
syntax	sentence structure	*Satzbau*
technical term	a word for a particular subject that is difficult to understand if you do not know about that subject	*Fachbegriff*
variety [vəˈraɪəti]	diversity, plurality; manner, kind, type	*Varietät; Vielfalt; Art*

Modern Media – Social, Smart and Spying?!

English word/phrase	explanation in English	German equivalent and/or synonym(s)
means of communication		
to access sth.; (to have) access to sth. ['ækses]	to find information, esp. using a computer; to have a computer, a car, etc. that you can use	*auf etw. zugreifen; Zugang (zu etw. haben)*
blog; blogger	web log, a web page containing information or opinions from a particular person or about a particular subject, to which new information is added regularly; sb. who writes a blog	*Blog (das, der); Blogger*
to broadcast (broadcast, broadcast)	to send out radio or television programmes	*ausstrahlen, senden*
cell phone	mobile phone	*Handy*
to communicate with sb.	to exchange information, news, ideas, etc. with sb.	*kommunizieren*
to connect; connected (to)	to join two or more things together; to be joined to a large system or network	*verbinden; verbunden (mit)*
cyberbullying ['saɪbəˌbʊliːŋ]	the activity of sending Internet or text messages to insult or threaten sb.	*Cybermobbing*
to design a website	to create or develop a website	*eine Internetseite erstellen*

Focus on Vocab

digital traffic	the number of people who have clicked or used a website	*Zahl der Besucher einer Website; Datenverkehr*
to distribute sth. via the Internet	to share things, e.g. news, among a group of people (using the Internet), esp. in a planned way	*etw. (über das Internet) verbreiten*
podcast	a digital medium consisting of a series of audio files users can download or stream to a mobile device	*Podcast (der)*
to post sth. online	to put sth. on a website	*im Internet veröffentlichen*
on the net	on the Internet	*im Internet*
(online) privacy ['prɪvəsi, *BE*; 'praɪvəsi, *US*]	the state of being free from the attention of others (when using the Internet)	*Privatsphäre im Internet*
to reply (replied, replied); reply	to answer; an answer	*antworten; Antwort*
to revolutionize sth.	to completely change the way that sth. is done	*umwälzen, revolutionieren*
search engine	a computer programme that searches the Internet for information	*Suchmaschine*
search term	a term/word which you enter in a search engine	*Suchbegriff*
to share	to let sb. have/use sth. that belongs to you; to tell others about your ideas, opinions, etc.	*etw. teilen; mitteilen*

smart phone	a mobile phone with an operating system	*Smartphone*
social networking (service)	a platform people can use to share their ideas and opinions and to stay in contact	*soziales Netzwerk(en); soziales Vernetztsein*
source of information	the place where sb. finds information	*Informationsquelle*
to subscribe	to pay money regularly to become a member of an organization, or to use a service regularly	*sich bei etw. anmelden; etw. abonnieren*
to text (message)	to send sb. a written message on a mobile device	*SMS schreiben*
wireless communication	a system of sending and receiving signals that does not use wires	*drahtlose Kommunikation*

English word/phrase	explanation in English	German equivalent and/or synonym(s)
electronic and digital media		
(targeted) advertising	the activity of telling the public about a product or service in order to persuade them to buy it (aiming at a particular group of potential customers)	*(gezielte) Werbung*
app(lication)	a software designed to perform operations on computers or mobile devices	*Anwendungssoftware*

audio file	a file on a computer in which sound data are stored	Audiodatei
to collect data	to gather information	Daten sammeln
compatibility [kəmˌpætəˈbɪlɪti]	the ability of computers and programmes to be used together	Verträglichkeit, Kompatibilität
computer-literate (*adj.*)	able to use a computer	sich mit Computern auskennen; wissen, wie man einen Computer bedient
data [ˈdeɪtə, ˈdɑːtə]	facts or information, esp. when examined and used to find out things or to make decisions	Daten
data preservation	the activity of storing data for later use or analysis	Vorratsdatenspeicherung
data protection	the act of guaranteeing that personally identifiable information is safe from being exposed	Datenschutz
data theft	the act of stealing data	Datendiebstahl
GPS	global positioning system	Globales Positionsbestimmungssystem
interactive media systems	media systems which allow information to be passed continuously and in both directions between the system/computer and the person using it	interaktive Medien

to invade sb.'s privacy	to affect sb.'s privacy in an unpleasant or annoying way	*in jds. Privatsphäre eindringen*
to spy	to secretly collect information	*spionieren, ausspähen*
to track sb.	to search for sb. by following the marks they leave behind them	*jdn. verfolgen*
to transfer data	to move information from one place to another	*Daten übertragen*
virtual	made, done, seen on the Internet or on a computer, rather than in the real world; artificial	*virtuell, nicht real, künstlich*
virus ['vaɪrəs]	instructions hidden in a computer programme, designed to cause faults or destroy data	*Computervirus*

English word/phrase	explanation in English	German equivalent and/or synonym(s)
online journalism		
24/7 news cycle (*infml.*)	when news stories are investigated and reported all day and all night long, at a very fast pace	*Nachrichten rund um die Uhr*
breaking news	a special report on an important topic, usually interrupting the regular programme	*Eilmeldung*
to comment on sth.	to express an opinion about sb. or sth.	*etw. kommentieren*

infographic	visual representation of data or information (charts, maps, etc.)	*Infografik*
news agency	an organization that collects news stories and supplies them to newspapers, radio stations, etc.	*Presseagentur*
newsfeed	a way of providing online readers with constantly updated news	*Nachrichten-einspeisung*
newsworthy	important or interesting enough to be reported	*berichtenswert*
paywall	a system asking readers to pay for content that is available online, e.g. on the website of a newspaper	*Bezahlschranke*
press coverage	when a subject or event is reported in the media	*Berichterstattung*
to quote; quotation	to repeat exactly what someone else has said or written; a sentence or phrase from a book, speech, etc. which you repeat e.g. in a piece of writing	*zitieren; Zitat*
short attention span	the period of time during which you continue to be interested in sth. is not very long	*kurze Aufmerksamkeitsspanne*

| sound bite | a very short part of a speech or statement, esp. one made by a politician, that is broadcast on a news programme | *kurzes, prägnantes Zitat* |

Find more vocabulary in the Student's Book on Focus on Facts, The Press (p. 370) and Focus on Facts, The Media (p. 325).

The British Empire

The system of triangle trading

British involvement with the **triangular trade began with the colonization of America in 1607 and the West Indies in 1623**. The chief British ports were London, Liverpool, Bristol and Glasgow.

Triangular trade is a historical term that refers to trade among three ports or regions and countries. The best-known triangular trading system is the **transatlantic trade** that operated from the seventeenth until the early nineteenth century, carrying manufactured goods, raw materials, cash crops – and slaves – between West Africa, the Caribbean and American colonies and the European colonial powers.

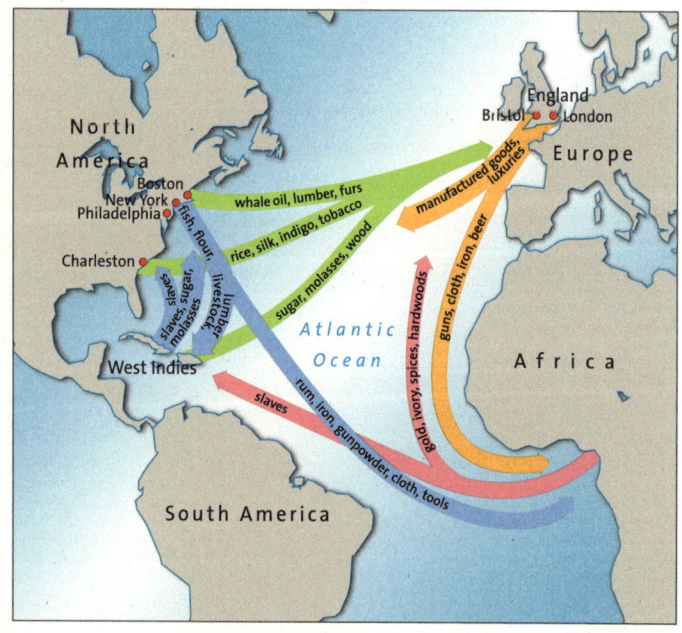

The **use of African slaves was fundamental** to growing crops such as cotton and tobacco, which were then exported to Europe. In turn, European goods were used to buy slaves from traders in Africa or the Caribbean. The slaves were transported to the Americas on the sea lane, the so-called middle passage, which was a horrible journey during which many slaves died of diseases and maltreatment. **Slave trade was started in 1501** by Portuguese and Spanish traders; in 1807, the UK Parliament passed a bill that officially abolished the trading of slaves, but there was still illegal slave trade across the Atlantic Ocean that was practiced until the second half of the nineteenth century. There are an estimated 27 million victims of slavery worldwide today.

The British Empire in 1750

The British Empire in the 1750s (the blue shaded areas) traded goods worth £17 million, £8.7 million in exports and £8.3 million in imports. Britain's trade grew enormously because Britain gained control over many different parts of the world. The wish for expansion and the need for raw materials during the **Industrial Revolution** caused a series of overseas wars among several European countries such as France, Spain and Holland. However, one of the first British trading companies, the **East India Company**, founded in 1600 during the reign of Elizabeth I, and the **Virginia Company**, founded by her successor James I, which was the basis for the first North American colony, the **Jamestown Colony in 1607**, formed the foundations of the growth and rise of the British Empire. Many colonies began as trading centres or were founded to protect a trade route, and were run for the profit of the mother country. The wealthiest area in the early days of the Empire was the **West Indies** due to large profits from sugar cane and tobacco. Slaves were brought to the West Indies to work on the plantations. The map shows the variety of goods that Britain imported from all over the world that greatly influenced the British economy and people's lives in the **mother country**.

The British Empire in 1900

Starting in 1801 the expanding empire was managed from London by the **Colonial Office**. District officers and civil servants were sent out to administer the colonies on behalf of Britain. Regular **imperial conferences** were held in Britain to discuss matters of general concern, such as trade, defence and foreign policy.

India was controlled for many years by the wealthy **East India Company**, roads and railroads were built to make trade easier, a **Governor-General** was put in charge, and British troops and civil servants were sent to the region. In 1858, following the Indian Mutiny, India was placed under the direct control of the British government and a **viceroy** replaced the Governor-General. British influence in India had expanded from a few trading stations into the **Raj** (= British rule). In 1876, **Queen Victoria** was proclaimed **Empress of India**. India brought Britain great wealth and strategic advantage, and was called the 'jewel in the crown of the Empire'. Local Indian rulers were allowed to remain in power provided they were loyal to the viceroy. Many British people spent years working in India as civil servants, engineers, police officers, etc. and took their families with them. The second period of empire-building took place in the late nineteenth century. The British Empire was at its largest and most powerful around 1920, when about 25 % of the world's population lived under British rule and over a quarter of the land in the world belonged to Britain. It was said that it was an empire **'on which the sun never sets'**, and the value of exports and imports was £970 million. At that time

The Brighton Pavillion was built in 'Hindoo' style in the early nineteenth century.

Britain was **one of the greatest economic and political powers in the world**. It was also thought by some people to be a moral obligation and destiny to govern poorer, less advanced countries and to pass on European culture to the native inhabitants. This was what Rudyard Kipling called the 'white man's burden'.

Britain did not only import foreign goods; there was also a great influence of foreign ideas, especially from India.

In the eighteenth century curry recipes and the famous 'mulligatawny soup' (the Tamil word for 'pepper-water') appeared in England. Indian designs influenced art and architecture, and polo, snooker and billiards, games which were played by British soldiers in India, were 'exported' to Britain.

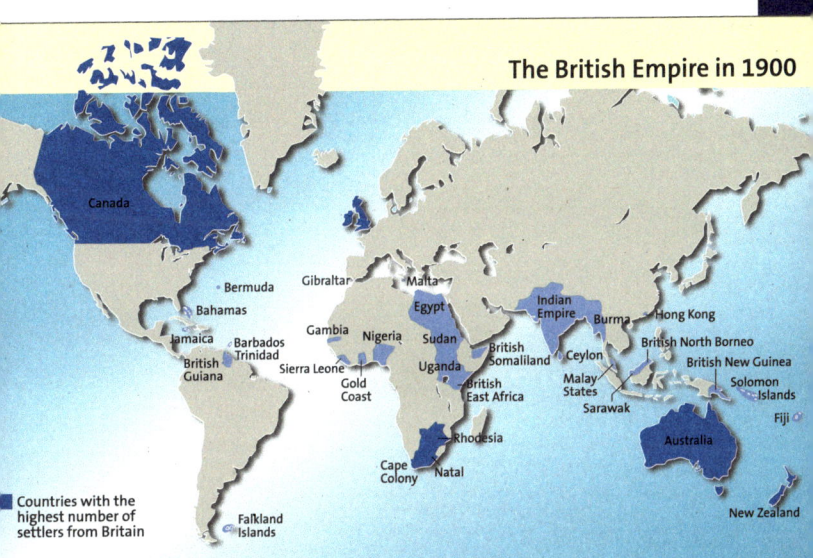

The Commonwealth of Nations

The Commonwealth of Nations is an **intergovernmental organization** of 54 independent member states. All but three of these states were formerly part of the British Empire. **The cooperation of these states follows a set of values and goals outlined in the Singapore Declaration of 1971 and the Harare Declaration of 1991**. The Head of the Commonwealth is a ceremonial and representative position held by the English king or queen, currently Queen Elizabeth II.

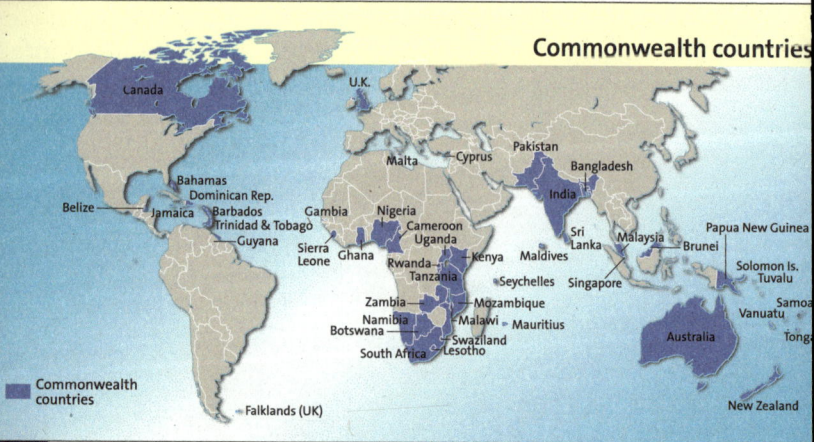

History

1926	in the **Balfour Declaration** at the Imperial Conference, Britain and its dominions agree they are equal in status, united by the common allegiance to the Crown and freely associated members of the **British Commonwealth of Nations**
1949	following the **London Declaration**, the word "British" is dropped from the title to reflect its changing nature (mostly politically independent member states)
1971	**Singapore Declaration**
1991	**Harare Declaration**
2003	**Aso Rock Declaration** states: "We are committed to democracy, good governance, gender equality, and a more equitable sharing of the benefits of globalisation."

Headquarters

The **Secretariat** was established in 1965 and is based in London; **headquarters** are in Marlborough House.

Members

The **54 current members** comprise all six inhabited continents, a population of 2.1 billion (= 1/3 of the world's population) and ca. 20 % of the world's trade. The three largest Commonwealth members are Canada, Australia and India.

Membership criteria include the promotion of (racial) equality, world peace, liberty, human rights and free trade.

Since 1939, every four years the **Commonwealth Games** are held, featuring the usual athletic disciplines as well as sports popular in the Commonwealth such as netball and rugby (2018: Gold Coast City, Queensland, Australia).

Great Britain – Immigration and Minorities

Immigration, minorities and ethnic groups

After World War II, Britain needed more workers and admitted citizens of Commonwealth countries without restriction. Many came from the Caribbean and from India, Pakistan and Bangladesh. They found work in hospitals, the textile industry and the public transport system, for example. **Nearly 500,000 Commonwealth citizens came to Britain before 1962**, many of whom were later joined by their families. When there were no longer enough jobs, the **Commonwealth Immigrants Act (1962)** was passed to restrict the number of immigrants entering Britain. In the following years, several more acts were passed. **Immigration is now strictly controlled.** Normally, only people from the European Union and certain Commonwealth citizens can get permission to live in Britain. Until the Brexit of 2016, Britain accepted about 50,000 immigrants every year.

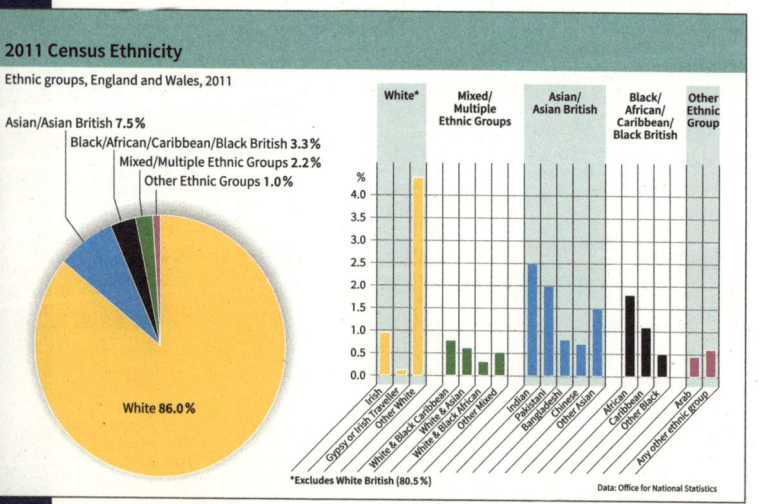

2011 Census Ethnicity

Focus on Facts

In order to control and systematize immigration, Britain introduced a **Points Based System (PBS)** in 2008, which categorizes non-EU citizens into five tiers according to their professional qualifications and background.

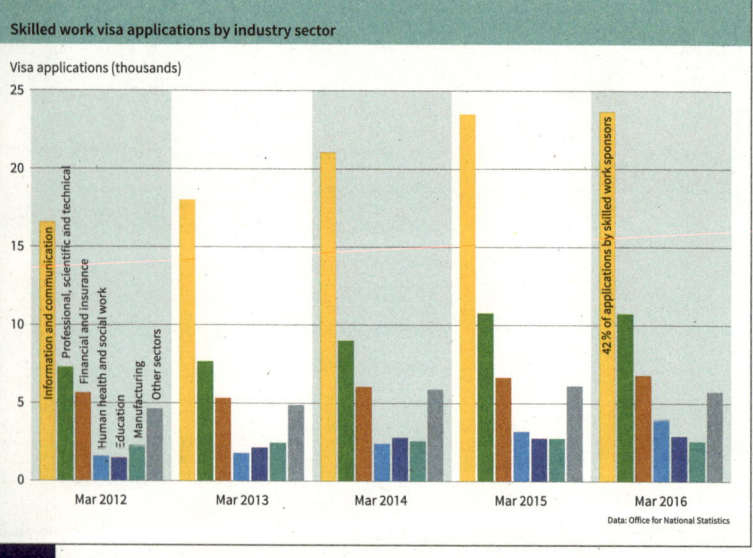

Skilled work visa applications by industry sector
Data: Office for National Statistics

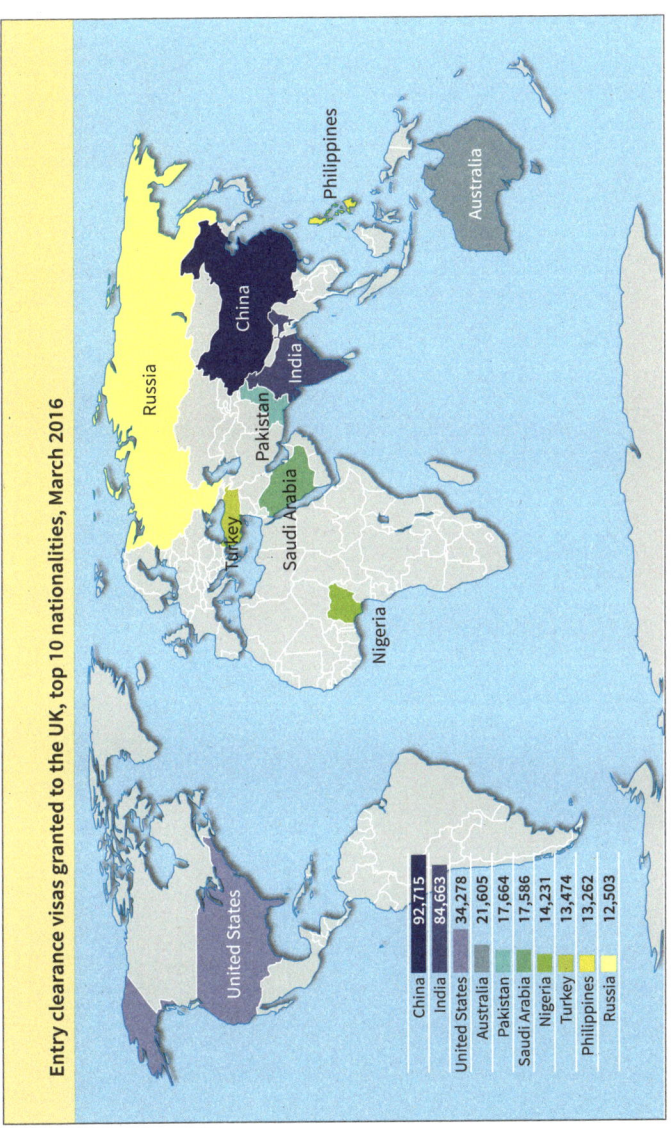

The European Union

The European Union (EU) is an **economic and political union** of 28 member states (ca. 505 million citizens) that has developed a single market **ensuring free movement of people, goods, services and capital**. The EU operates through supranational and intergovernmental negotiations and treaties between the member states. Economically the EU generates ca. 25 % of the gross world product.

History

1957	**Rome Treaty** creates the European Economic Community (EEC) as a customs union. Members: Belgium, France, Italy, Luxembourg, the Netherlands, West Germany
1979	first direct democratic elections to the **European Parliament**
1985	**Schengen Agreement** creates open borders without passport control between most member states
1986	the European flag is first used
1990	after German reunification, (former) East Germany joins the community
1993	in the **Maastricht Treaty**, the European Union is formally established
2002	the **Euro** is introduced as European currency and replaces national currencies in twelve of the member states
2016	23 June: 51.9 % of Britons vote in favour of leaving the European Union (→ Brexit)

Fundamental rights

- In 2009, the **Lisbon Treaty** gave legal effect to the **Charter of Fundamental Rights of the European Union** which is a catalogue of fundamental (human) rights which were derived from the constitutional traditions of the member states (e. g. **Article**

1: Human dignity is inviolable. It must be respected and protected; **Article 2:** Everyone has the right to live. No one shall be condemned to the death penalty, or executed).

Important EU institutions

- the **European Council** is the EU's supreme political authority; it defines the EU's political agenda and strategies
- the **European Commision** is the EU's executive branch and responsible for its legislation
- the **European Parliament** (in Strasbourg) forms half of the EU's legislature; the members of the European Parliament are directly elected by the EU citizens every five years
- the **Council of the European Union** is the other half of the EU's legislature; in addition to legislative functions it also has executive functions, e. g. the Common Foreign and Security Policy
- the **Court of Justice of the European Union** interprets and applies the treaties and the law of the EU
- the **European Central Bank** administers the monetary policy of the 18 member states taking part in the **Eurozone**; it is one of the world's most important central banks

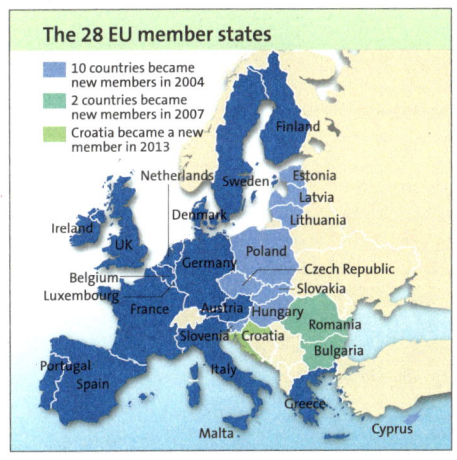

The Political System of the United Kingdom

The **United Kingdom** (of Great Britain and Northern Ireland) is **a constitutional monarchy**, in which the **monarch is the head of state and the Prime Minister is the head of government**. The UK has been a multi-party system since the 1920s, the two largest parties being the Conservative Party and the Labour Party.

Political parties

The Conservative Party	Labour Party 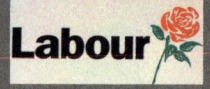
• centre-right • conservatism • British Unionism (against Scottish and Welsh independence) • opposition to the Euro, strong defense of Pound Sterling • Eurosceptic position • free-market policy • criticism of Labour's state multiculturalism	• left to centre-left • democratic socialist party • supports government intervention in the economy • for redistribution of wealth • advocates increased rights for workers • favours an extended welfare state • support of multiculturalism

The debating chamber of the British House of Commons in the Palace of Westminster, London

The U.K. system of government (separation of powers)

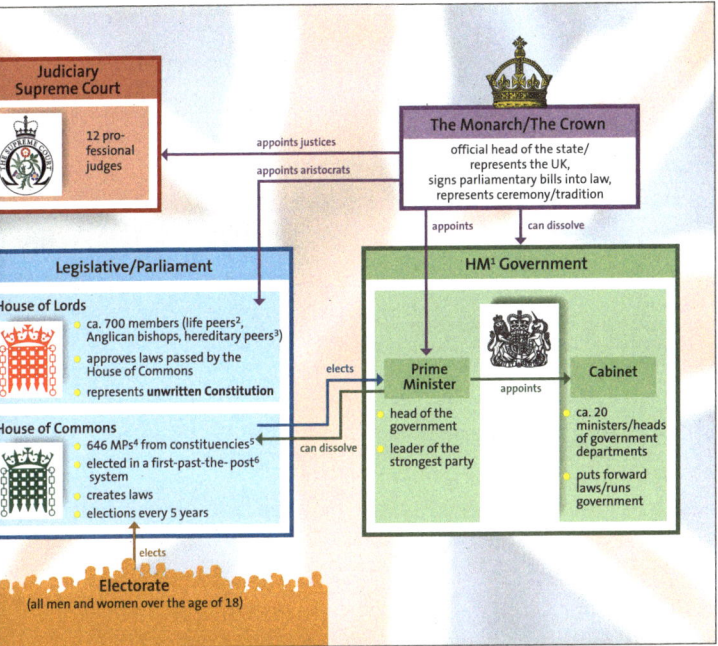

---

[1] **HM** (*abbr.*) Her/His Majesty's – [2] **peer** in Britain, a person who has a high social position and any of a range of titles, including baron, earl, and duke, or a life peer – [3] **hereditary peer** [həˈredɪtəri] someone who became a peer (= a high social rank) when a parent died, and who can pass it onto their oldest child; *Mitglied des Hochadels mit ererbtem Titel* – [4] **MP** (*abbr.*) Member of Parliament – [5] **constituency** [kənˈstɪtjuənsi] *Wahlbezirk* – [6] **first-past-the-post** system using a voting system in which a person is elected because they get more votes than anyone else in the area that they want to represent; *einfache Mehrheitswahl*

India: From Raj to Modern Democracy

With its 1.18 billion people, India, officially **the Republic of India**, is the second-most populous country in the world and the world's largest democracy. In its long history, India has always been known for its commercial and cultural wealth and diversity. Today India is a federal constitutional republic with a parliamentary democracy and consists of 28 states and 7 union territories. Head of State is the President of India, but the most executive power is exercised by the Prime Minister, who is also the head of government.

India is considered to be one of the fastest-growing economies in the world and well known for its pluralistic, multilingual and multi-ethnic society and its commercial and cultural wealth and diversity.

India's national emblem, the Lion of Sarnath, third century B.C.

India's flag, the Tricolour, with the navy blue wheel with 24 spokes (= Ashoka's Dharma Chakra). Each spoke depicts one hour of the day and portrays the prevalence of righteousness all 24 hours.

History

Third cent. B.C.	**Ashoka the Great** unites most of South Asia
320 – 550 A.D.	A.D. the **Gupta dynasty** is considered to be the **Golden Age of India**; extensive inventions and discoveries were the foundation of the **Hindu culture**
1526 – 1857	age of the **Mughal Empire**
16th cent.	European powers establish trading posts
1616	the **British East India Company** is founded
1856	the British East India Company controls most of India

1857	**Indian Mutiny:** native soldiers employed by the British Army rebel against racial injustice and inequities; as a consequence civilian rebellions follow → the East India Company is dissolved and India is directly governed by the Crown → **British Rule/Raj**
1885	the **Indian National Congress** is founded and developed into one of the largest democratic political parties in the world; it is a major force in the struggle against British rule in India
1920s	the Indian National Congress adopts **Gandhi's ideas of non-violent civil disobedience and resistance**, which later leads to the **Quit India Movement** which is also led by Gandhi
1947	the **Indian Independence Act** leads to the dissolution of the British Indian Empire
15 Aug. 1947	India gains independence; **Partition of India** into two independent states: the **Dominion of Pakistan** (later Islamic Republic of Pakistan and People's Republic of Bangladesh) and the **Union of India** (later Republic of India)
1948	**Mahatma Gandhi is assassinated** by a Hindu fanatic
1948/1965/ 1971/1999	**Indo-Pakistan wars** over disputed territory in Kashmir and Jammu
1974	first **nuclear test explosion** under the codename "Smiling Buddha" (five further tests in 1998)
1991	economic liberalization and major reforms initiated by Prime Minister Rajiv Gandhi
2005	the **Right to Information Act**
2009	the **Right to Education Bill** provides free and compulsory education for children between 6 and 14
2013	the **National Food Security Act** aims at providing subsidized food grains to ca. two thirds of India's population; beneficiaries can buy 5 kg per eligible person per month of cereals like rice, wheat or millet (*Hirse*); pregnant women, lactating (breastfeeding) mothers and certain categories of children are eligible for daily free meals

Facts and figures: Modern India

Name	Republic of India
Capital	New Delhi
Area	3,287,590 square km
Population	1.237 billion (2012)
Growth of population	1.58 % p. a. (2014) (Germany: –2.7 %; 2011)
Life expectancy	68.89 years (Germany: 80.89; 2012)
Child mortality	44 deaths (per 1,000) (Germany: 3.8)
Official languages	17 major languages (e.g. Hindi, English, Telugu, Assamese, Urdu, Santali, Punjabi, Bengali, Tamil) + 844 dialects
Literacy rate	74.04 % (men: 82.14 %; women: 65.46 %) (Germany: 99 %)
Religions	Hinduism 80.5 %, Islam 13.4 %, Christianity 2.3 %, Sikhism 1.9 %, Buddhism 0.7 %, Jainism 0.5 %
Government type	Sovereign Socialist Democratic Republic with a Parliamentary system of Government
National days	**26 January – Republic Day**; 15 August – Independence Day; 2 October – Mahatma Gandhi's birthday
GDP[1] by sector	service: 64.8 %; agriculture: 13.7 %; industry: 21.5 % (2013) (Germany: 69.0 %; 0.8 %; 25.5 % (2013))
GDP per capita	$1,504 (2013) (Germany: $45,097; 2013)
GDP growth	4.7 % (2013) (Germany: 3.2 %; 2013)
Population below poverty line	22 % (data: Reserve Bank of India, 2012) 14.3 % (data: World Bank, 2014) (Germany: 15 %; OECD, 2014)
Main industries	telecommunications, IT, textiles, chemicals, pharmaceuticals, food processing, steel, transportation equipment, cement, mining, petroleum, machinery
Natural resources	oil, natural gas, coal (ca. 10 % of world's coal reserve), iron, bauxite, titanium, chromite, etc.

Share of top eight investing countries in FDI[2] inflows in 2014

Rank	Country	Inflows (Million USD)	Inflows (%)
1	Mauritius	78,527	36%
2	Singapore	25,445	12%
3	U.K.	20,764	10%
4	Japan	16,268	8%
5	USA	11,927	6%
6	Netherlands	11,236	5%
7	Cyprus	7,446	3%
8	Germany	6,519	3%

dipp.nic.in/English/Publications/FDI_Statistics/2014/india_FDI_March2014.pdf

---

[1] **GDP** (*abbr.*) Gross Domestic Product; *Bruttoinlandsprodukt* –
[2] **FDI** (*abbr.*) Foreign Direct Investment

American Beliefs and Values

Although there have been significant shifts in societal concepts and traditions, the following ideals, beliefs and values continue to be some of the most important in American culture.

Fundamental, inalienable and God-given rights

- **Liberty:** personal and religious freedom
- **Pursuit of happiness:**
  - (personal and material) success and wealth
  - optimism and belief in "anticipated success"
  - individuality/individual ways of pursuing one's dreams and realizing one's goals
- **Equality:** equal rights for men and women/equal rights for people from different ethnicities and social backgrounds
- **Life:** leading a secure life protected by the law, government and military

Patriotism

- importance of **national symbols** (e.g. the Statue of Liberty, the Declaration of Independence, the Constitution, the U.S. flag, the National Anthem, etc.)
- strong identification with one's nationality and **pride in being American**

Puritanism/Protestant work ethic

- the **Puritan belief that hard work, thrift, discipline, self-improvement and responsibility** lead to worldly success and prosperity and that this is a sign of God's benevolence and grace
- continuous and active participation in society and entrepreneurial endeavors
- believing that one is exceptional, **a member of "God's chosen people"**, following a divine providence (→ **Manifest Destiny**)

- belief in authority as a means of protecting the personal rights of the people

The American Dream

- the phrase "American Dream" was first expressed by the American historian and writer **James Truslow Adams in 1931**, describing a set of complex beliefs, promises of religious and personal freedom and opportunities for prosperity and success, as well as political and social expectations
- its basic underlying concept has roots in the **Declaration of Independence of 1776** which refers to basic human rights such as **"Life, Liberty and the Pursuit of Happiness"** which are **"inalienable"** and God-given and based on the assumption that "all [people] are created equal"

An open and dynamic society

- being generally open to new ideas and inventions (→ progress)
- being generally open to immigrants of any nationality, provided they contribute positively to the country
- different concepts of how to integrate immigrants:
  a) the **melting pot** image: people are "melted together", i.e. they are expected to give up their original culture and identity and are "transformed" into a homogeneous "American culture"
  b) the **salad bowl** image: national, ethnic and cultural patterns/habits are kept distinct by the immigrants while they are rather loosely integrated into the "American culture"

→ SB, Focus on Documents,
The American Dream, p. 139

An Uncle Sam wind wheel toy for children

The Civil Rights Movement: Fighting for Freedom and Equality

The **peak years of the American Civil Rights Movement** were the **1950s** and **1960s**, when African-Americans kept demonstrating and fighting for human and civil rights, thus forcing the U.S. government **to guarantee** them certain **constitutional rights**, e.g. the right to vote and to attend public facilities like schools, buses or restaurants together with white Americans.

However, African-Americans have been struggling to overcome slavery and racial injustice since the 17th century and famous leaders and activists like **Sojourner Truth** (1798–1883), **Booker T. Washington** (1856–1915), **W.E.B. Du Bois** (1868–1963) and **Frederick Douglass** (1817–1895) paved the way for "modern" activists like **Martin Luther King Jr.** (1929–1968) and **Malcolm X** (1925–1965).

June 1623	the **first eleven slaves** arrive in New Amsterdam (New York)
1863	President Abraham Lincoln signs **Emancipation Proclamation** that officially abolishes slavery
1865	• 15 April: **President Lincoln is assassinated** by a fanatical Confederate • the **Thirteenth Amendment** to the Constitution **abolishes slavery** by law; more than 4 mio slaves gain freedom "Neither slavery nor involuntary servitude ... shall exist within the United States, or any other place subject to their jurisdiction."

1865/66	the **Black Codes**, a set of rules, are passed in the South to "restore all of slavery but its name"; southern blacks are • denied the right to vote • restricted from moving freely • denied the right to own land • excluded from certain jobs • subject to a separate and much more severe penal code • prohibited from possessing firearms
1866	the **Ku Klux Klan** is founded in Tennessee as a fraternal organization opposed to the emancipation of the blacks; white southern "aristocracy" fears "nigger domination" and aims at restoring white supremacy in the South; terrorist acts against blacks like lynching are carried out
1868	the **Fourteenth Amendment** affirms **black citizenship**
1870	the **Fifteenth Amendment** guarantees blacks **the right to vote**
1870s	**racial segregation** is gradually enforced in the **American South**
1890	Louisiana passes a law enforcing **"equal but separate"** access to colleges, trains, etc.
1880s–1920s	peak years of black **lynchings**
1910	**NAACP** (National Association for the Advancement of Colored People) is founded; the U. S.'s oldest civil rights organization
1920s	the **Black Muslims**, later the Nation of Islam, promotes the separation of blacks from white Americans
WWI	**segregated regiments** of white and African-Americans fight for the U. S.
WWII	ca. 1 mio African-American soldiers fight for the U. S.
1955/56	• **Rosa Parks** is arrested in Montgomery, Alabama • **Montgomery bus boycott** • 26-year-old Baptist Reverend **Martin Luther King Jr.** begins active participation in the civil rights movement
1957	the **SCLL** (Southern Christian Leadership Conference) is founded to support the protest movement; leader: Martin Luther King Jr.

1960s	- **Malcolm X** becomes famous leader of **Black Muslims**; promotion of a separate black state and acceptance of violence as a means of self-defense
- **Freedom Riders**: black and white civil rights activists travel through the segregated South to peacefully protest against racial segregation → Gandhian philosophy of non-violent resistance
- **sit-ins** at segregated lunch counters in southern towns
1961	January: **John F. Kennedy** is elected **President** of the U. S.
1963 – 1965	- Martin Luther King Jr. leads **marches from Selma to Montgomery**; civil rights activists march peacefully for the African-Americans' right to vote
- 28 August: **March on Washington**; 250,000 people listen to **Martin Luther King's famous speech "I have a dream"**, delivered in front of the Lincoln Memorial in Washington D. C.
- 23 November: **assassination of John F. Kennedy** in Dallas, Texas
1964	- President Lyndon B. Johnson signs **Civil Rights Act**, ensuring voting rights to African-Americans
- **Freedom Summer**: a campaign to register as many African-American voters in the state of Mississippi as possible
- **revival of the Ku Klux Klan** in Mississippi
1965	- 21 February: **assassination of Malcolm X**
- President Lyndon B. Johnson signs **Voting Rights Act**; literacy tests required to be allowed to vote are suspended in order to allow many illiterate southern blacks to vote
1965 – 1968	- **Black Power Movement**; stronger political focus; urban protests
- **Black Panthers**: culminating frustration; radicalization; guns; urban protests
1967	Martin Luther King launches **Poor People's Campaign**: economic protest and civil disobedience of rural and urban poor of all races

1968	- 3 April: **Martin Luther King is assassinated** in Memphis, Tennessee - eruption of violence in 125 cities nationwide
1992	April: **riots in Los Angeles** following the beating of African-American Rodney King by white policemen
1995	October: **Million Man March** to Washington D.C. organized by the Nation of Islam to promote "unity, atonement, and brotherhood"; more than 250,000 participants
2008/2012	**Barack Obama** becomes **first African-American President**
2012/2014	- public protests following the killing of unarmed African-American teenagers - 26 February 2012: 17-year-old African-American teenager **Trayvon Martin** is shot by a Hispanic security officer in Sanford, Florida - 9 August 2014: 18-year-old African-American student **Michael Brown** is shot by a white police officer in Ferguson, Missouri
2016	- 5 July: Alton Sterling, a 37-year-old black man, is shot by white police officers in Baton Rouge, Louisiana - 6 July: Philando Castile is shot by a St. Anthony, Minnesota police officer; his girlfriend livestreams a video of the shooting on Facebook - 7 July: at the end of a peaceful Black Lives Matter protest, African-American Army Reserve Afghan War veteran Micah Xavier Johnson, 25, shoots five police officers in Dallas, Texas - in response to these shootings, civil unrest and protests are held in New York, St. Paul, Minnesota and Baton Rouge, Louisiana; at least 261 people are arrested

Lincoln Memorial in Washington D.C. being cleaned by an African-American worker

The United States: Immigration and Minorities

The English have been going to North America from the late 16th century on; Spain sent people to the southern part of the region and many Dutch and Germans also went over. When the U.S. became independent, it was written into the **Constitution** that there could be no limits on immigration until 1808. The main period of immigration was between 1800 and 1917. Early in this period, many immigrants arrived from Britain and Germany, and many Chinese went to California. Later, the main groups were Italians, Irish, Eastern Europeans and Scandinavians. Many Jews came from Germany and Eastern Europe. Just before World War I, there were nearly a million immigrants a year. Most Americans have a clear idea of what life was like for the immigrants: they left home because they were poor and thought they would have better opportunities in the U.S. Many immigrants came to New York and Boston, and **Ellis Island**, near New York, became famous as a receiving station. The **Immigration Act of 1917**, and other laws that followed it, limited the number of immigrants and the countries that they could come from. Since then, immigration has been limited to a few people who are selected for an **immigrant visa**, commonly called a **green card**. Hispanics and Asians now make up the largest groups of immigrants. **The Immigration and Naturalization Service** (INS) is responsible for issuing visas. It also tries to prevent people from crossing the borders and entering the U.S. illegally.

In 2013, a bipartisan (*aus Mitgliedern beider Parteien bestehend*) group of eight Senators ("The Gang of Eight") announced four basic principles for a comprehensive immigration reform:
- a citizenship path for illegal immigrants already in the U.S.
- business immigration system reforms

- an expanded and improved employment verification system
- improved work visa options for low-skill workers and an agricultural worker programme

On 27 June 2013, the U.S. Senate approved the "Border Security, Economic Opportunity, and Immigration Modernization Act of 2013" (short "S.744"). However, so far the bill has ended in deadlock in the U.S. House of Representatives.

Ethnic minorities in the USA (U.S. census of 2010)

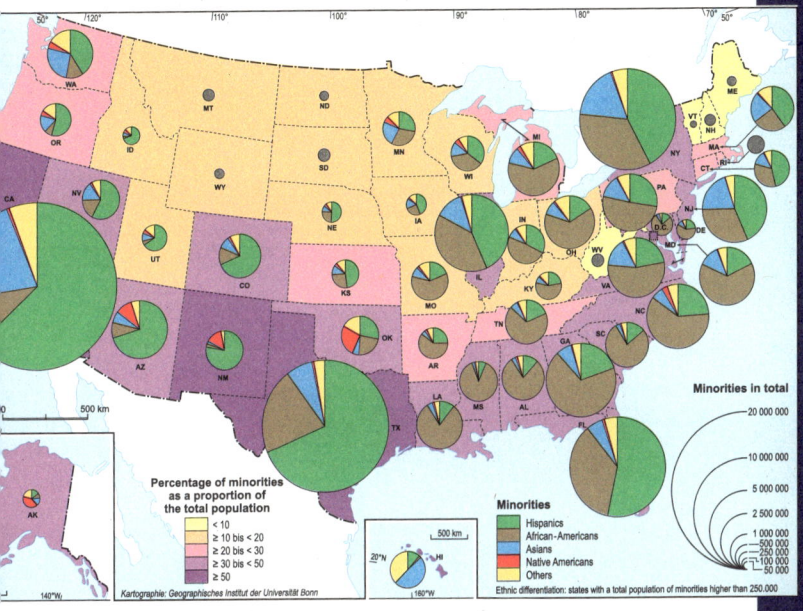

The Political System of the United States

The U.S. system of government (checks and balances)

The United States Constitution demands a **separation of power**. Each branch of government exercises power over each of the other branches. This prevents any one branch from becoming too powerful.

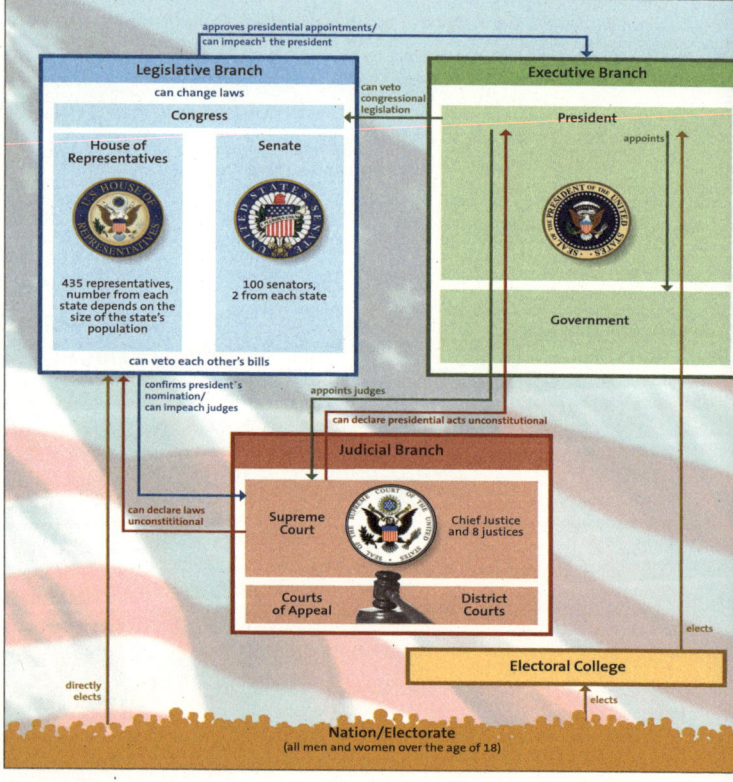

---

[1] **to impeach a president** (US) *ein Amtsenthebungsverfahren*

The United States has a **first-past-the-post voting system** in which the highest polling candidate is given all the votes and elected. Most states require citizens who wish to vote to be **officially registered**. Every **legal citizen over the age of 18**, regardless of ethnicity or gender, **has the right to vote**. Voting is carried out by **free and secret ballot**[1], in which the voters cast a **ballot (paper)** in a **ballot box** or via (electronic) **voting machines** in **polling places**, or via mail ballots.

Political parties

In 1787, America's founders expected constitutional provisions such as the separation of power, checks and balances, federalism and indirect election of the president by an electoral college[2] would deter[3] the formation of parties. However, **in 1800 the U.S. became the first nation to develop organized political parties** which had executive[4] power. Since the 1860s, the Republican and Democratic parties have dominated American politics. In a 2006 Gallup Poll, ca. 59 percent of Americans identified themselves as either Republicans or Democrats.

Those people claiming to be independent normally have partisan[5] leanings[6].

---

[1] **ballot** *Wahl, Abstimmung* – [2] **Electoral College** a group of people who come together to elect the President and Vice-President, based on the votes of people in each state – [3] **to deter sb.** [dɪˈtɜːr] *abschrecken* – [4] **executive** [ɪgˈzekjʊtɪv] the part of a government that is responsible for making certain that laws and decisions are put into action – [5] **partisan** strongly supporting a person, principle, political party – [6] **leaning** *Tendenz, Neigung*

Democratic Party	Republican Party
• evolved from the party of Thomas Jefferson, formed before 1800 • is considered to be more liberal • believes that government has an obligation to provide social and economic programs • favours a higher taxation of the rich • has a stronger obligation to environmental engagement	• was established in the 1850s by Abraham Lincoln and others who opposed slavery • is considered to be more conservative • tends to believe that social and economic programs are too costly to taxpayers • encourages private enterprise • believes that a strong private sector makes citizens less dependent on government

The election process

- the U.S. Constitution stipulates[7] that **a presidential election is to be held once every four years**
- in February of the election year, the parties nominate candidates in so-called state primaries[8] and caucuses (*U.S., Gremium, Ausschuss*)
- at national party conventions, usually held in the summer, **state delegates vote for the party's presidential candidate**
- on election day (usually the first Tuesday following the first Monday in November) every citizen has an opportunity to vote in **a process of indirect popular election known as the electoral college**, in which the number of electors is based on the population of the state

---

[7] **to stipulate** (*fml.*) to state clearly and firmly that something must be done, or how it must be done; schriftlich vereinbaren –
[8] **(state) primary** *Vorwahlen*

- these electors assemble following election day, cast their ballots and officially select the next president
- the Constitution mandates[9] that **Senators be elected directly by the voters of their state** once every six years
- the **members of the House of Representatives are also elected directly by the voters** of their state every two years

The inauguration[10] of the president

- the president-elect and the vice president-elect **take the oath of office** and are inaugurated on 20 January
- over the years, the inauguration has been expanded to a daylong event, including the oath-taking[11] ceremony, parades, speeches and balls
- traditionally, the sworn-in president delivers a speech, the so-called **inaugural address**, in which he inspires hope for the future and outlines fundamental plans and objectives[12]

"I ... do solemnly swear that I will faithfully execute the office of President of the United States, and will to the best of my ability, preserve, protect, and defend the Constitution of the United States."

---

[9] **to mandate** to order sb. to do sth. – [10] **inauguration** [ˌɪnɔːɡjʊˈreɪʃən] the ceremony in which sb. is put into an official position – [11] **oath-taking** *den Amtseid ablegen* – [12] **objective** *(politisches) Ziel*

The Colonization and Decolonization of Africa

The race for Africa in the nineteenth century

At the end of the nineteenth century (1881–1914) a **period of new imperialism and expansionism** led to an **imperial rivalry** among the European nations. As a consequence, Africa was rapidly claimed and divided up between the European powers, who eventually gained total control over the continent and its people. Famous European explorers such as David Livingston (1813–1873) and Serpa Pinto (1845–1900) laid the foundation for the **growing interest in Africa's resources and territories**.

Reasons for overseas expansion includes:
- developing lucrative markets
- investments outside Europe (railway, telegraph, infrastructure, etc.)
- enlargement of territories and possessions
- military and naval bases
- demand for raw materials (resource extraction)
- African coasts as stopover ports
- strategic overseas trade and waterways
- anthropology (scientific study of races)

@ Further information and maps depicting European imperialism and the partitioning of Africa from the 17th to the 20th century are provided on the webcode.

The end of colonial rule

The end of the First and especially the Second World War marked the collapse of the European empires, which led to the gradual process of decolonization and, finally, the independence of the African colonies.

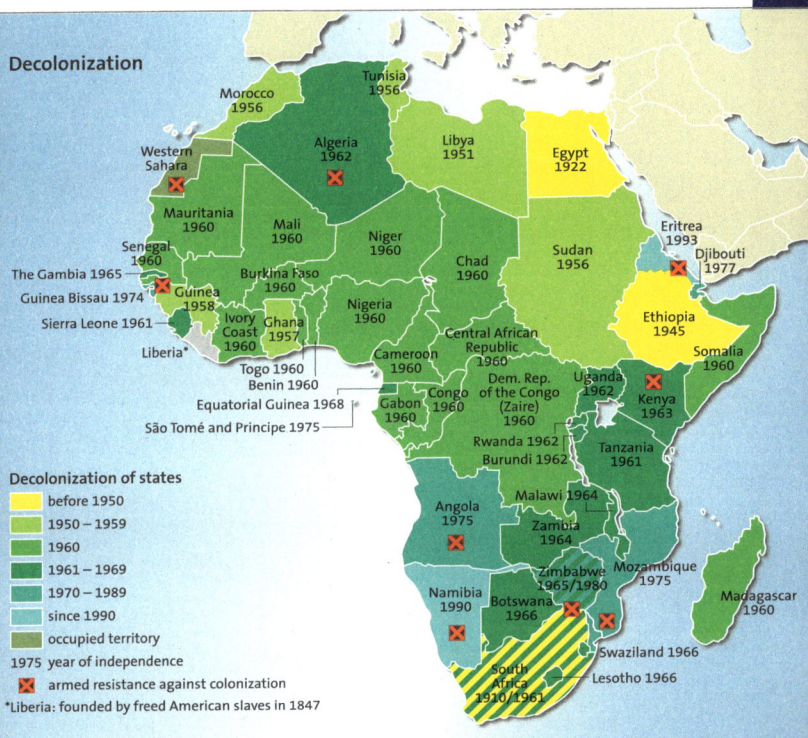

Progress & Responsibility in a Global World

The three historical periods of globalization

- **exploration (until 1500)**
  - founding and forming of villages, cities and infrastructure
- **colonization (1500 – 1900)**
  - development of writing and printing technologies (e.g. the Gutenberg printing press)
  - the Industrial Revolution (1750 – 1830)
  - advances in communications (e.g. telephone, telegraph)
- **internationalization (1900 – present)**
  - international trade and organizations (e.g. WTO (World Trade Organization), IMF (International Monetary Fund), World Bank, United Nations)
  - technology and global media (e.g. satellite, computers, Internet, WWW)
  - information revolution (e.g. personalization of communications → social networks, etc.)

Risks and opportunities

risks	opportunities	future tasks & requirements
- rising competition - increasing (inter-)dependencies - control by multinationals - uncontrolled money flow - growing inequalities - widening social gaps - environmental degradation	- diffusion of new ideas, technologies, products, services, lifestyles - new potential markets and customers - increase of communication - increasing coherence of politics in economy, society	- thinking globally → locally <u>and</u> globally - being prepared to venture into the unknown - developing intercultural competencies - being prepared for crosscultural encounters - being future-oriented a sustainability

- degradation of social standards
- widening power imbalances
- concentration of multinational companies

- and employment due to international standards
- global information network and exchange
- cooperation through partnerships

- developing production and service skills
- developing flexibility
- getting access to information

Components of globalization

environment
- ecology
- global warming
- deforestation
- pollution
- efficient use vs. plunder of resources

culture/society
- education
- language
- shift of norms & values
- Westernization
- tourism
- change of lifestyles

economy
- production
- work
- trade
- markets
- consumption

technology
- scientific & technological advancement
- modernization
- information
- health care

population
- decline (rich countries) vs. expansion (poor countries)
- migration
- overpopulation
- outsourcing
- diseases (e.g. AIDS, HIV)
- ageing

media
- communication
- information
- surveillance

politics
- UN agencies
- NGOs
- NATO

World Trade

World Economic Forum

The **World Economic Forum** (WEF), founded in 1971, is a Swiss nonprofit foundation that meets annually in Davos, and **brings together international business and political leaders, intellectuals and journalists to discuss pressing global issues**.

Besides its economic focus, the annual meeting has become a neutral platform for political leaders to resolve political differences. In 2008, Microsoft founder Bill Gates gave a keynote speech on "creative capitalism", which combines generating profits and solving the world's inequities by using market forces to address the needs of the poor worldwide. The participants are considered a global elite – a think tank of internationally-oriented experts, including a group of "Young Global Leaders" consisting of under-forty-year-old leaders from all around the world and representing a wide range of disciplines and sectors.

WEF has also **launched several global initiatives**, e. g. the **Global Health Initiative**, the **Global Education Initiative** and the **Partnering Against Corruption Initiative**.

However, there is heavy criticism as well: WEF, along with the G8 and the World Trade Organisation, are viewed as a "mix of pomp and platitude" by anti-globalisation activists and many NGOs.

Further economic forums

- **The Group of Eight (G8):** France, Germany, Italy, Japan, the United Kingdom, the United States, Canada and Russia

This group has occasionally been expanded, e. g.:

- **Outreach Five (O5):** plus Brazil, China, India, Mexico and South Africa
- **Group of Twenty (G20):** the 20 major economies of Africa, North America, South America, East Asia, South Asia, Southeast Asia, Western Asia, Eurasia, Europe and Oceania; the group meets semi-annually, and the last meeting took place in Hamburg in July 2017.

Global players – and the consequences

- **multinational companies** (or mega corporations) play an important role in the international economy: they often have powerful influence on local economies, international relations and even politics (→ lobbying)
- **many multinational companies are criticized** due to lax environmental standards, bad labour standards (e. g. sweatshops in developing countries, control of tariffs → unfair wages), marginalization of local businesses/markets
- many multinationals hold **patents** (e. g. Siemens, Adidas) in order to prevent the rise of competitors
- examples of **influential multinational corporations** are: ExxonMobil, Wal-Mart, McDonald's, General Electric, Boeing, Microsoft and British Petrol
- the United Nations declare **2005 the International Year of Microcredit**; microloans are designed to spur entrepreneurship in developing countries and gain acceptance in the mainstream finance industry as a source of future growth

The United Nations

The **United Nations Organization** (UNO, UN) was **founded in 1945 to replace the League of Nations** in order **to stop wars** between countries and as **a platform for international dialogue**. It contains multiple subsidiary organizations with diverse functions to carry out the UN's missions. Today, about 192 nations belong to the UN. When nations become a member of the UN, they agree to accept the obligations of **the UN Charter**, which states the **four basic purposes of the UN**:

- to maintain **international peace and security**
- to develop **friendly relations among nations**
- to be a centre for **harmonizing the actions of nations**
- to cooperate in **solving international problems** and promoting **respect for human rights**

The organization of the United Nations

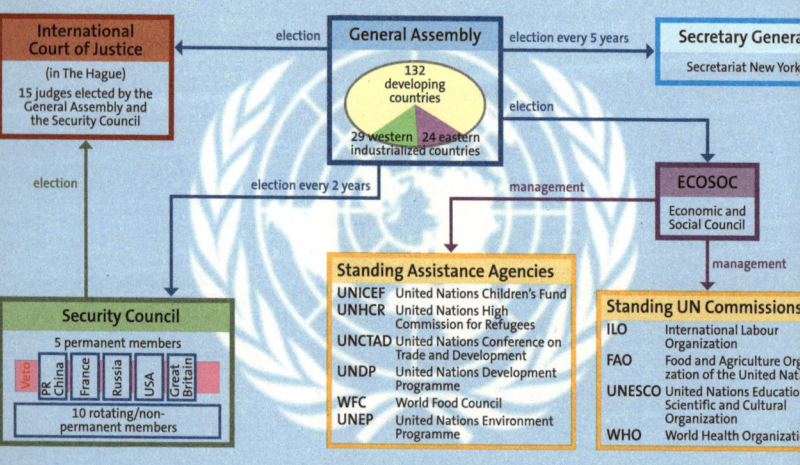

Global issues on the UN Agenda

- Africa
- Ageing
- Agriculture
- AIDS
- Atomic Energy
- Children
- Climate Change
- Culture
- Decolonization
- Demining
- Development Corporation
- Persons with Disabilities
- Disarmament
- Drugs and Crime
- Education
- Elections
- Energy
- Environment
- Family
- Food
- Governance
- Health
- Human Rights
- Human Settlements
- Humanitarian and Disaster Relief Assistance
- Indigenous People
- Information Communications Technology
- Intellectual Property
- International Finance
- Iraq
- Labour
- International Law
- Oceans and the Law of the Sea
- Least Developed Countries
- The Millenium UN General Assembly – The Goals
- Questions of Palestine
- Peace and Security
- Population
- Refugees
- Science and Technology
- Social Development
- Outer Space
- Statistics
- Sustainable Development
- Terrorism
- Trade and Development
- Volunteerism
- Water
- Women
- Youth

www.un.org/issues

Sculpture in front of the UN headquarters in New York

Genetic Engineering

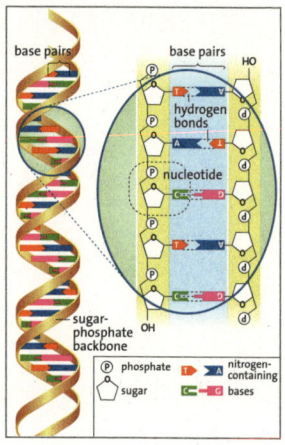

Genetic engineering (or genetic modification) is the **human manipulation of an organism's genetic material** to create a genetically modified organism that does not exist under natural conditions. During this process, new genetic material (DNA) is inserted into the host genome (= the entirety of an organism's hereditary information). First the **genetic material of interest is isolated and copied**, thereby generating a construct that contains all the necessary genetic elements, which is then **inserted into a host organism** in a second step.

Thus, **genetic engineering changes the genetic design or genetic blueprint of an organism** and **forms new combinations** of heritable (= *erblich*) genetic material. Although **stem cell research** and **cloning** are not considered to be genetic engineering by definition, these areas of scientific research are closely connected to genetic engineering because they can be used together.

In **medicine** genetic engineering is used e. g. for **the mass production of insulin, human growth hormones, follitism (for treating infertility) and vaccines**. Researchers are also working to genetically engineer humans and e. g. **replace defective humans genes with functional ones** and thus **cure genetic disorders and diseases** like Parkinson's disease, cancer, diabetes, heart diseases and arthritis.

Despite all the (possible) benefits of genetic engineering there are also **ethical concerns and criticism** that this technology is not only used for treatment but for enhancement, modification or alteration of a human being's character, behaviour, appearance, intelligence or adaptability.

Historical development

Year	Major scientific discovery or achievement
1856–63	Austrian monk and scientist **Gregor Johann Mendel** (1822–84) shows that the inheritance of certain traits follows particular laws (the **"Laws of Inheritance"**); "father of modern genetics"
1953	American zoologist **James Watson** and British physicist **Francis Crick discover the double helix**, the chemical structure of DNA
1972	American biochemist **Paul Berg creates the first recombinant** (= altered, modified) **DNA**
1974	German biologist **Rudolf Jaenisch creates a transgenic mouse** by inserting foreign DNA into its embryo
1976	Genetic Engineering Technology Inc., **the first biotechnology company, is founded in California** by U.S. businessman Robert A. Swanson and biochemist Dr. Herbert Boyer
1978	Genentech Inc. **produces genetically engineered human insulin**
1980	the **U.S. Supreme Court rules that genetically altered life can be patented**
1986	first field trials in the **USA and France: genetically engineered tobacco plants** are resistant to herbicides
1992	**China commercializes virus-resistant tobacco plants**
1994	the **first genetically-modified tomato**
2000	**completion of the first draft of the human genome**
Feb 2001	first analyses of the public and private genome projects are published; the big discovery: **Humans have about 30,000 to 40,000 genes, hardly more than a common weed or worm**
April 2003	the **human genome is declared a finished product**; the 50th anniversary of the discovery of the double helix
2008	Craig Venter announces first synthetic organism controlled by a **completely synthetic chromosome**
1996–2001	increasing **commercialization of biotech crops** at a growth rate of 8 % (1.7 mio hectares in 1996 – 160 mio hectares in 2011; corn, soybean, cotton)
2013	production of a **synthetic yeast** (*Hefe*) **cell with 16 artificial chromosomes**; creation of **genetically-engineered mice with artificial human chromosomes** in every cell of their bodies

The Media

In the domain of communication, **media** are tools used to store or transmit information and/or data. The term **mass media** or **public media** is used to describe the sum of mass distributors of news and entertainment. These media include **print media**, **electronic media**, and **digital media**. Gutenberg, who perfected the printing press with movable types in 1454, is considered the inventor of "print media". Today, modern communication media facilitate so-called **"many-to-many communication"** (e. g. via e-mail or Internet forums), whereas more traditional media typically represent **"one-to-many communication"** (e. g. TV, radio, cinema). Generally, the purpose of mass media is to promote businesses and their products by providing entertainment, information and socially-relevant services.

Impact and influence of the media

advantages/positive effects	risks/dangers/negative effects
• effective and quick exchange of information • possibility of being interconnected supports people in authoritarian states, e. g. the Arab Spring of 2011 – "democratization" process • giving public access to hidden/withheld information • (almost) unlimited access to information even in remote places, e. g. developing countries • exchange of cultural and social values • achievement of social control (e. g. public polls, citizen journalism) • platforms for individual presentations and contributions	• influencing politics and public opinion • spying and surveillance (e. g. domestic wiretapping; *Telefonüberwachung*), datamining, etc. • publishing secret information (e. g. WikiLeaks) • influencing children and teenagers (e. g. exposure to violence, role models, advertising, etc.) • creation of an illusionary world (e. g. through soap operas – escapism) • imbalance of information (e. g. developed vs. developing world)

Tools of media and types of communication

digital media
- Internet (websites)
- e-mail
- mobile phone
- blogs (web logs)
- vlogs (video logs)
- RSS feeds
- podcasts
- QR code
- video games
- social networking
→ digital distribution

print media
- books
- newspapers
- magazines
- catalogues
→ from the late 15th century
→ physical distribution

broadcast/ electronic media
- radio (ca. 1910)
- recorded music (late 19th century)
- film/cinema (ca. 1900)
- TV (ca. 1950)
- discs (1908s), tapes (1920s)
- e-book (1990s)
- podcasts
- e-publishing
→ electronic distribution

public communication
- TV
- newspapers/ magazines
- social networking
→ many-to-many communication

personal communication
- telephony
- mail (post)
- mobile phones
→ person-to-person communication

Focus on Facts

Basic Types of Fictional Texts

Focus on Skills

| 1. narrative texts | **a) Novels**
• are an extended and complex work of fiction written in prose.
• contain a variety of characters, action and a greater complication of plot.
• present a sustained exploration of the milieu, the characters, their motives.
• can vary greatly in form, style and content; one less complex form is the novella (e. g. John Steinbeck, *Of Mice and Men* or *Cannery Row*).
• have certain subclasses, e. g. the social novel (e. g. Harriet Beecher-Stowe, *Uncle Tom's Cabin*), the coming-of-age story (e. g. Mark Twain, *Tom Sawyer and Huckleberry Finn*, Paul Auster, *Moon Palace*).

b) Short stories
• are written in prose and are shorter and less complex than a novel.
• are mostly confined to one setting, a limited number of characters and events.
• often employ an open plot with an abrupt opening and ending.
• do not put focus on the development of a character but on a significant incident or decisive moment that reveals strengths and weaknesses of characters, mostly presented as a snapshot of life.
• are told from the point of view of a narrator who is created by the autor.
• place maximum significance on the few things mentioned, which are aimed at producing a certain effect on the reader's mind.
• emerged in the USA in the 19th century in response to the development of the newspapers, which required shorter forms of text; Edgar Allan Poe (1809–1849) is often regarded as the originator of the short story; other famous writers of short stories include Ernest Hemingway, Annie Proulx, and T.C. Boyle.

c) Fables
• are a short text in which animals represent human types (→ the beast fable). |

1. narrative texts	- are a form of allegory exemplifying an abstract moral thesis or principle of human behaviour. - are didactic and are intended to teach the reader a moral lesson. - Two famous writers of fables are James Thurber and George Orwell.
2. dramatic texts	**a) Dramas/plays** - are any work designed for performance in a theater. - require actors/actresses who take on the roles of different characters, performing the actions and speaking the dialogue or monologue. - mostly contain stage directions included by the playwright, telling the actors how and where to move on stage as well as giving information about how to arrange the stage, what props, sound effects or lighting to use. → Focus on Facts, Drama and Theatre, pp. xxx **b) Screenplays/scripts** - are a written work, especially for a film or a television programme. - consist of numbered scenes which show action and dialogue descriptions. - have numbered slug lines telling the reader that the story has changed in location and time (e.g. INT. WAREHOUSE – NIGHT; EXT. STREET – DAY).
3. poetry/ lyrics	**a) Poetry** - is a type of literature that is not prose, in which ideas, experiences and feelings are expressed in compact, imaginative and often musical language. - may be arranged in lines and may contain patterns of rhyme/rhythm. - often contains figures of speech and imagery to appeal to the readers' and listeners' emotions and imagination. **b) Lyrics** - are a set of words that accompany music, either spoken or sung. → Focus on Skills, Analysis of Poetry and Lyrics, pp. 378

Basic Types of Non-Fictional Texts

The 4 basic types of non-fictional texts

1. Descriptive texts: the author wants to inform in a relatively balanced and neutral way (e.g. description of a landscape, a place, a person, an object …)

2. Narrative texts: the author wants to inform the reader about a development or a sequence of events; the report (objectively or subjectively) gives answers to the questions *who? what? where? when? why?* and *how?* and often presents further details. Reports* are often made livelier by fictional elements, e.g. a detailed description of people or the way people are affected by an event, etc. (e.g. travel report, report on the development of a situation …)

3. Expository texts: complicated and difficult facts are presented and explained in a matter-of-fact way; the structure pattern of such texts is called **topical order** (= a sequence of points follows a statement of the topic at the beginning of the text (e.g. explanatory notes, scientific reports, factual texts, descriptions of historical events …)

4. Argumentative texts: the author tries to influence the reader directly; this text type tends to be more critical and appellative, using persuasive arguments (e.g. commentary, criticism, review*, essay*, sermon*, pamphlet, political speech* …); these texts mostly deal with controversial topics; reasons are advanced for and/or against the matter and are arranged in a well-planned order

Forms of argumentative texts

structure	type 1	type 2	type 3
introduction	Presenting a topic and giving opinions on the problem	Presenting a topic and giving opinions on the problem	Presenting a topic and giving opinions on the problem
↓	arguments ↓	arguments ↓	arguments ↓
main part	supporting facts	counter-arguments and refutation to stress the author's position	argument → counter-argument argument → counter-argument argument → counter-argument, etc. [mainly used in disputes and debates]
↓	↓	↓	↓
conclusion	conclusion	conclusion	conclusion

A non-fictional text* that puts forth a personal view has a **unity of thought**, and usually follows a clear structure (line of thoughts*, train of thought*, line of argument*).

Here are some of the most common **compositional patterns for structuring texts**:

listing structure:	method:	Enumerating, numbering of facts, ideas, arguments
	effect:	Clarity and coherence through parallel arrangement
progressive structure:	method:	Using a clearly-defined starting point; developing on a cause-to-effect or problem-solution arrangement
	effect:	Clarity through unity and logical coherence
antithetical structure:	method:	Contrasting and juxtaposing of facts, ideas and arguments
	effect:	Clarity and emphasis through comparison and contrast

Understanding Complex Texts

A text can be "complex" for different reasons:
- It is a **historical document** or a **historical play** (e.g. Shakespeare) that contains words with a different spelling and meaning than in contemporary English (e.g. "thee", "thou" → Elizabethan English).
- A **legal text** which is written in formal English and contains many technical terms.
- The text is **very long** and does not have obvious paragraphs.
- The text has a **scientific topic**, is written in formal English, employs technical terms/academic language.
- The (literary) text contains a lot of **implicit meaning** (e.g. figurative language, symbols, allusions, etc.), lapses in time (*Zeitsprünge*), multiple points of view, etc.
- The text **requires a lot of life experience** from the reader (e.g. cultural, historical, literal background knowledge, etc.) and expects the reader to "read between the lines" to understand the underlying references.

Step 1: Before reading
- Read the headline of the text and try to **anticipate what the text will be about**. Take notes and/or make a mind map of the topic, the plot or possible arguments the text might deal with.
- If the text is about a scientific/historical topic, you can **do some research in advance** to get a first overview of the matter.
- If the text is fictional, e.g. a play or novel, try to **get information on the respective topic** of the text and/or the author/playwright first.

Step 2: While reading
- Be prepared to **read the text at least twice**:
  - in a **first reading**, try to get a **general understanding**
  - in a **second reading**, focus on **details in connection with the assignments** you are given.
- **Annotate the text** and **use different colours** for different aspects.

- **Highlight** or **underline** relevant information, e. g.
  - names of people/places
  - special vocabulary/ technical terms
  - statistical data/numbers
  - main ideas/arguments
  - unknown vocabulary
  - references/allusions

  Tip: Do not underline whole sentences but focus on essential keywords or arguments, etc.
- **Make notes in the margin.** For example:
  - Divide the text into paragraphs/thematic units.
  - Write a summarizing headline or sentence of each paragraph/thematic unit.
  - Write your own definitions or explanations of difficult terms
  - Translate ideas into your own words (paraphrasing); use a dictionary if necessary.
  - Ask questions about aspects you do not understand or you are critical about.
  - Distinguish between information/facts given and personal remarks or evaluations made in the text.
  - Comment on ideas/arguments of the author or thoughts/dialogues of characters in a play/novel.
  - Identify the message of the text and the author's intention.

Tip: Make sure that you have **understood the assignments correctly** and focus on the aspects you are required to examine, to explain or to comment on or evaluate.

Step 3: After reading

- **Sort and structure your notes** (e. g. by numbering them) and make sure that you do not distort (*verfälschen*) the information given in the text.
- **Use your pre-reading** research on the matter and cross-check the information given in the text. You can use it for your evaluation or analysis as well.

Analysis of a Fictional Text

The 3 basic types of fictional texts

a) **Narrative texts** (e.g. novel, short story, fable)
b) **Dramatic texts** (e.g. drama/play, screenplay/script)
c) **Poetry/lyrics**

Step 1: Analysis of the general meaning

- Identify and specify the type of text as well as the theme/topic/subject of the given text.
- Answer the W-questions: who, what, where, when, why?
- Write a summary of the given text of about 150–200 words at the most.
- Identify the narrator and specify what point of view is being used to tell the story.
- Develop a first (general) evaluation of the meaning and message of the text.

Step 2: Analysis of basic elements

a) **Identify the structural and narrative/stylistic devices** and show **what effect and function** they have.

The following grid contains some terminology and tips for your analysis. The most relevant vocabulary can be found in the Literary Terms Section.

narrator, narrative situation, point of view, mode of presentation	first-person narrator, witness/observer narrator, third-person narrator, objective/reliable narrator, subjective/unreliable narrator, limited point of view, unlimited/omniscient point of view, panoramic presentation, scenic presentation, relation of acting time and narrating time

structure	• (How) is the text structured? • What time span does the narration cover? • What is the relation between acting time and narrating time? • Which conflict is the story based on? • How does the action develop – or stagnate? • Are there any leitmotifs?
characters	flat/round characters, protagonist vs. antagonist, minor character(s), hero(ine), anti-hero, outward appearance, behaviour, relationship to other characters, direct or indirect characterization
setting (= time and place)	scenery, mental climate, basic mood, social environment, atmosphere • Does the scenery/setting itself imply any symbolism? (e.g. thunderstorm = danger, large city = liveliness, anonymity, etc.) • What is the effect on the audience? • What intention might the author/playwright have had?
language/ style	level of speech, manner of speaking, style, syntax, choice of words, inner monologue, chain of associations, stream of consciousness, register

b) Never forget to quote from the text to demonstrate the correctness and accuracy of your work.

Step 3: Comment on and evaluation of the text

- Classify and evaluate the text and its message.
- Relate the given text to other texts of the same epoch/time and/or compare it with other texts by the same author that you have dealt with. Pay attention to striking similarities and/or differences.
- Critically comment on the text and finish with a concluding sentence.

Note: Explanations of the respective terms can be found in the Literary Terms section, Students' Book, pp 405 ff.

Analysis of a Film Scene

General tips on viewing and analysing a film

- Watch the film scene at least two times.
- Work systematically and concentrate on the devices employed in the scene in a certain order.
- Take notes while or immediately after each viewing of the film scene.
- Whenever you identify and specify a certain narrative technique and/or cinematic device used in a film scene, explain and illustrate its function and effect on the viewer.
- In order to explain the use and function of cinematic devices precisely and correctly, make use of technical terms.
  → Literary Terms section, Students' Book, pp. 405 ff., and Focus on Facts, Camera Operations, Students' Book, pp. 372 f.
- When viewing and analysing a film scene, it is not possible to explain and demonstrate every single detail; therefore, you should focus on the most striking and relevant devices employed in the scene.

Step 1: Focus on narrative techniques

guiding elements	function
• **setting**: What is the time and place of the action?	→ orientation for the viewer
What is the atmosphere like?	→ general exposition
• **plot:** What happens and why?	→ drawing the viewers into the action, evoking and raising interest
• **suspense**: Which questions are raised and remain unanswered?	→ evoking the viewers' curiosity and keeping them interested
• **appearance of characters**: What do(es) the character(s) look like?	→ evoking interest, sympathy, antipathy, etc.

- **body language**: What is/are the character(s)' movements, gestures, postures, facial expressions?
→ revealing character traits, quirks, etc.
- **language/communication**: What choice of words and tone do(es) the character(s) use? How do they interact?
→ exposition of the intellectual background, demonstration of the characters' relationship(s)

Step 2: Focus on cinematic devices

cinematic device	function
• **camera operations**: Which field sizes, camera angles, camera positions, camera movements, etc. are employed?	→ transferring narration into film/images/pictures
• **visual symbols**: Which visual symbols (e. g. cross, blood, tombstone, eagle) are employed?	→ visual leitmotifs serve as links and help to express/to intensify a deeper contextual meaning
• **film music/sound**: What kind of music/what (background) sounds are employed?	→ to show/emphasize a mood, to create suspense, to foreshadow, etc.
• **(special) effects**: What further effects (e. g. slow motion, voice-over narration) are employed?	→ to intensify the action, to reveal thoughts, to suggest speed, etc.

Step 3: Explanation of the function of the scene (in the context of the film)

- Place the scene in the context of the film.
- Explain and give examples of how the scene
    a) moves the action forward and creates suspense,
    b) presents an unexpected turning-point in the action,
    c) reveals a new character trait of the protagonist,
    d) introduces (a) new character(s),
    e) defines (a) relationship(s) between characters.

Analysis of a Screenplay

A screenplay or film script is a written work for a film or TV programme. Basically, a film script depicts the **movement, actions, expressions and dialogues of characters** and gives **technical directions and instructions**, e. g. concerning the camera operations. The "action" is always written in the present tense. Here are further characteristic features of film scripts that you should consider in your analysis.

"Whatta you mean 'minor script changes?' It's supposed to be a western."

Format and style

- A screenplay **focuses on what is audible and visible** on screen.
- Screenplays have a **specific layout and codified[1] notations[2]** of technical or dramatic elements, e. g. scene transitions[3], changes in the narrative perspective, sound effects, emphasis on dramatically relevant objects, emphasis on characters speaking from outside a scene. These notations are always **written in capital letters**.
- **Different scene elements** are visualized by **tab settings[4]**, e. g. dialogue, scene headings, transitions or parentheticals[5].
- The **beginning** of a scene is usually marked with "FADE IN:", the **ending** with "FADE TO BLACK."

Slug lines[6]

One of the **most relevant and unique features** of screenplays are slug lines; they are always written in **capital letters** and are usually divided into three parts.

---

[1] **to codify** *festschreiben* – [2] **notation** *Bezeichnung* – [3] **transition** *Übergang* – [4] **tab setting** *Tabellator* – [5] **parenthetical** *Einschub* – [6] **slug line** a line of abbreviated text; master scene heading

Part 1 … determines the **general setting** of a scene, e.g. inside (interior = INT.) or outside (exterior = EXT.).
Part 2 … determines the **location** of the scene, e.g. SUSAN'S APARTMENT – KITCHEN, JIMMY'S CAR, etc.
Part 3 … determines the **time** of the scene, e.g. DAY, NIGHT, DAWN, LATE NIGHT, etc.
If a character starts inside and then walks outside during a scene, a new slug line is needed which begins with CONTINUOUS.
Examples: ● INT. ALICE'S HOME – BATHROOM – NIGHT
● EXT. PARK – DAY/MORNING
Further characteristics:
- each slug line begins a new scene
- slug lines are numbered consecutively
- any change of time or location requires a new slug line
- slug lines are on their own lines, flush with the left margin and are completely typed in capital letters.

Common abbreviations used in scripts

ELS	extreme long shot	2-S or 3-S	two-shot or three shot	VO	voice-over
MLS	medium long shot	INT	interior	OSV	offscreen voice
LS	long shot	EXT	exterior	DIS	dissolve
MS	medium shot	BG	background	MIC	microphone
MCU	medium close-up	POV	point of view shot	VTR	videotape
CU	close-up	ZI or ZO	zoom in or zoom out	ANNCR	announce
ECU	extreme close-up	SOT or SOF	sound on tape or sound on film	SUPER	superimposition
OS	over-the-shoulder-shot	SFX or F/X	special effects (sound or visual)	Q	cue

→ Focus on Facts, Screenplays and Storyboards, Students' Book, p. 369

Analysis of a Non-Fictional Text

Step 1: Analysis of structure and content

- Identify and specify the theme/topic/subject* of the given text.
- Identify the characteristics of the heading* (e.g. provocative, ironical, funny, etc.).
- Divide the text into parts and relate these parts to the heading and the whole text.
- Write a summary of 150 words at most.
- Determine the message of the text. Predict the basic characteristics of the text (type).
- Clarify the line of argument, the train of thought* (general structure of the text).

Step 2: Analysis of stylistic devices/use of language

a) **Identify the stylistic devices** and show their effect and function. The following grid contains vocabulary for your analysis. Most relevant vocabulary (marked with *) can be found in the Literary Terms Section, Students' Book, pp. 405 ff.

register (= *Sprachebene*)	slang, colloquial, everyday English, written language, (in)formal, poetic, sophisticated, familiar, technical terms, scientific, religious, metaphorical
choice of words	denotations*, connotations*, keywords, figurative*/literal meaning of words, emphatic/negative function of words, euphemisms*, synonyms*, abstractions
style	plain, sober, natural, matter-of-fact, clear, precise, concise, vigorous, fluent, passionate, elegant, artificial, stilted, wordy, colourless, cliché-ridden, snappy, lengthy, clumsy, spontaneous, trite, expressing doubt/certainty
tone	humorous, playful, colloquial, conciliatory, depressive, serious, solemn, ironical, satirical, sarcastic, warm-hearted, aggressive, whining, reproachful
rhetorical devices	alliteration*, anaphora*, allusion*, reference*, antithesis*, ellipsis*, hyperbole*, irony*, metaphor*,

rhetorical devices	paradox*, personification*, simile*, symbol*, understatement, exaggeration*, parallelism*, employment of leitmotifs*, repetitions*, juxtapositions*, (rhetorical) questions*, quotations, enumerations*, appeals, comparisons, digressions from the main topic, grammatical tenses, illustrations, superlatives, personal pronouns (we – they, I – you, our – their, us – them)

b) **Don't forget to include quotes** to demonstrate the correctness and accuracy of your work. This is ow to do it:
- When **referring** to an important part of the text without quoting the words, give the page(s) and/or line(s): e.g. *Obama tells the audience about his jogging with foreign students (ll. 15 – 19).*
- You can **integrate the quotation** into your sentence: e.g. *Obama is determined to establish "an environment of lifelong learning" (l. 54), which means that …*
- You can **use a full quotation**: e.g. *Obama starts with the most important point: "First, to help every child begin school healthy and ready to learn." (l. 42).*
- Note the abbreviations:
  - one page or line: p. 5/l. 5
  - more pages or lines: pp. 2 – 5/ll. 2 – 5
  - the following page(s), line(s): f./ff. (e. g. pp. 5 f. or ll. 10 ff.)

  Note: **Omissions** of any kind are indicated by […]. Remarks or **changes from the original text** are indicated by squared brackets: *He* [Obama] *says …*

Step 3: Evaluation of the text

- State whether (or not) the text is well-structured/convincing/effective/appropriate …
- Discuss if/to what extent the text/author is able to address the reader(ship).
- Critically comment on the text, and refer to similar texts that you have dealt with.
- Finish with a concluding sentence.

Analysis of Poetry and Lyrics

Poetry (from the Greek "poiesis" = making, creating) is a type of literature in which **ideas, experiences and feelings are expressed** in compact, imaginative, and often musical language. Poets arrange words in ways designed to touch readers' senses, emotions and minds. Lyrics are a set of words that accompany music, either by speaking or singing. The word *lyric* derives from the Greek word "lyrikos" (= a song sung by the lyre). Most poems and lyrics are written in lines that may contain patterns of rhyme and rhythm to help convey their meaning. They often use **figures of speech and imagery to appeal to the readers' and listeners' emotions and imagination**. The poet or songwriter usually invents a speaker from whose point of view the feelings, ideas, experiences, etc. are expressed. Poems and songs may be divided into stanzas (groups of lines) or sections and can greatly vary in structure, theme and atmosphere.

general meaning/ content	<ul><li>What situation/topic is presented?</li><li>What is the theme; are there any (striking) leitmotifs?</li><li>What is the author's/singer's intention; what is the message of the poem/song?</li><li>What kind of register of English has been chosen (poetic, colloquial, archaic, slang, etc.)?</li><li>What is the melody like (harmonious, rhythmical, tuneful, staccato, etc.)?</li></ul>
formal analysis: a) structural devices	<ul><li>Examine – the structure of the poem/song (stanzas, lines, (lack of) punctuation, refrain(s), break(s), enjambements, chorus, etc.) – the use of repetitions and/or enumerations/parallelisms – the use of contrast(s)/antithesis – the use of an illustration (= an example to make an idea clear) – the rhyme scheme (e.g. pair rhyme aa bb cc; cross rhyme abab; enclosed rhyme abba) – the use of free verse.</li></ul>

b) sense devices	– (How) are objects and ideas/thoughts brought together? – What type(s) of sentence(s) is/are used (hypotactical/paratactical sentences, questions, commands, etc.)? – Are there allusions/references to a certain topic (e.g. nature, city, love, etc.)? – Check on the use of simile (a direct comparison: "like, as"), metaphor (an implied comparison without a connective word: "an ocean of tears"), personifications (something nonhuman is given human characteristics: "the frosty cliffs looked cold"), or symbols (an object that also stands for some abstract idea: a red rose → symbol of love, beauty). – the use of grammatical tenses – the speaker's point of view – the employment of hyperbole/exaggeration
c) sound devices	• Examine – the use of alliteration/anaphora, – the use of rhymes and/or assonances (= imperfect rhymes), – the use of a particular rhythm, beat, – the use of onomatopoeia (= words that imitate a sound: buzz, cuckoo, etc.), – the instrumentation, beat, vocal/instrumental type of music, vocals, etc. → **Show how these devices support, stress/emphasize the meaning/content of the poem/song (→ function/effect).** → **Show how style and content are connected.** → **Show how sound and lyrics match and support each other.**
d) final comment and evaluation	• Try to classify the given poem/song (refer to other poems/songs by the same author or authors of the same background). • Evaluate the poem/song (Is the poem/song convincing? Has the author/singer succeeded in conveying his/her message? etc.). • What do you consider to be the final message of the poem/song? • What do you consider to be the effect on the reader/listener?

Analysis of a Political Speech

General aspects of political rhetoric

The purpose of most political speeches is persuasion rather than information. There is always a (hidden, underlying) message involved, often related to certain attitudes and values of the speaker. A political statement intends to affect the listeners by making use of diverse structural and rhetorical devices. In order to understand and to be able to evaluate a political speech, one should consider the following aspects:

first (general) impression:	• topic, subject matter, general tone, issues and purpose of the speech
contents and structure:	• salient and striking topics, important aspects • organization of the text, arrangement of parts (e.g. introduction, main part or body, conclusion) • train of thought, composition, line of argument
circumstances of the speech/ political context:	• time and place/medium (e.g. TV, radio, face-to-face, Internet) • position of the speaker (president, leader of a political party, leader of a protest movement, etc.) • audience (mass audience, a limited group of people) • occasion (election campaign, protest demonstration, political debate, informal gathering) • genre and type (presidential address to the nation, sermon, speech at a demonstration, campus speech, testimony)

formal and stylistic devices:	
a) language	• keywords and phrases • word groups/clusters related to a certain topic • different registers for different addressees (e. g. sophisticated language to address rich and/or educated people, use of dialect, etc.) • choice of words (colloquialisms, slang expressions, poetic expressions)
b) grammar	• sentence structure/syntax (use of main-/subclauses) • use of grammatical tenses (indirect references to history, future, etc.)
c) rhetoric	• use of rhetorical questions and answers • use of contrast and oppositions (positive/negative, familiar/alien, near/distant, etc.) • use of key symbols, slogans, stereotypes • abstractions and generalizations • use of grammatical persons (I, us, we – you, they: patterns of identification and solidarity or vice versa) • metaphors, personifications • allusions and references to history (American Dream, important political/historical issues, good/bad times, tradition, future, etc.); quotations • repetitions (alliterations, anaphora); parallelisms • comparisons, numbers, factual information • irony, exaggerations, simplifications • imperatives, emotionally-loaded words • concentration on essential points vs. wordy • insertions
d) manner of speaking/voice	• volume, tempo, stress, intonation, abrupt changes, pauses, rhythm
evaluation:	→ Comment on the personal integrity of the speaker, the general political circumstances, the impact on the listeners. → Compare the speech/speaker to other political speeches/speakers. Was he/she convincing?

Analysis of Statistical Data

different types

	1992	2001	2020
USA	230 mn	260 mn	300 mn
China	800 mn	1,000 mn	1,300 mn
India	600 mn	800 mn	1,100 mn

A table gives raw data as the basis for analysis and consists of a grid with numbers arranged in lines and columns. Typically, it aims to present data in an ordered way, thus making the information easy to understand.

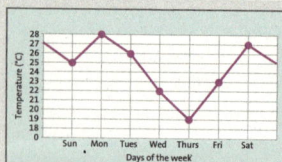

A (line) graph presents one or more lines in a system of coordinates/axes – a horizontal and a vertical axis. It shows the development of figures/variables over a period of time (trends, tendencies).

general aspects

- How reliable/trustworthy is the source?
- Are the numbers up-to-date?
- Consider why a chart/graph/table has been chosen as the means of visual representation.
- Are the figures absolute numbers or percentage figures – and what is the function of this presentation?
- What do the numbers/data suggest?
- Turn the percentage figures/data into words and compare them.
- Relate the data to the given context.

useful terms and phrases

■ to reach a peak/a low point/an all-time high/low of … ■ to remain constant/stable ■ to go through a period of growth ■ to increase/rise/grow/go up ■ to decrease/fall/drop/go down ■ a fall/decline/drop/decrease ■ an increase/a rise/growth ■ to grow … by 10 %/at a certain rate ■ a rise of 8 %/in temperature/to €25 ■ steep/strong/rapid … growth ■ a gradual/steady/continual … fall ■ a slight/barely noticeable … rise

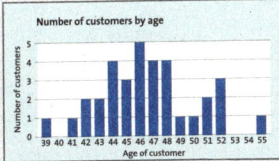

A bar chart shows differences between various things. It presents boxes/bars of different heights in a system of coordinates. The bars can be arranged horizontally or vertically.

useful terms and phrases

■ in comparison with/compared with ■ in contrast to ■ to achieve an average/below-average/above-average figure ■ to be at the top/bottom of the ranking ■ to rank first/second … last ■ the highest/lowest figure/score ■ no/little/a big difference between A and B (… with regards to … last year …) ■ the figures are identical/similar to … ■ the vast majority of/only a minority … ■ to experience a sudden rise/drop ■ after a brief recovery …

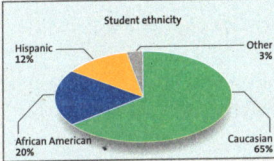

A pie chart shows percentages of a whole. It consists of a circle/pie divided into different sections/segments.

useful terms and phrases

■ the pie chart is divided into … ■ segments/sections ■ each segment represents … ■ the share of 5 % of the total amount is about 2 million euro … ■ the biggest/the smallest section ■ the whole circle represents/stands for … ■ the chart reveals the share of … ■ percentage-wise ■ a marginal percentage of … ■ an infinitely small amount of

Analysis of Visuals

Visuals or images can be all kinds of graphical material, e.g. photos, film stills, adverts, paintings, etc.

Analysis of cartoons

A **cartoon** is a **comic or satirical drawing** in a newspaper, a magazine or on the Internet that aims at humorously criticizing current, and especially political, events. It usually consists of a drawing (**pictorial part**) and speech balloons and a comment or a caption (= a short title), which is most frequently placed underneath (**textual part**). However, all the elements are not necessarily used in each cartoon.

Step 1: Author and source
- What is the title or caption of the cartoon?
- Which artist drew the cartoon (if known)?
- Where was the cartoon published (newspaper, magazine, Internet, etc.)?

Step 2: Descriptive level
- Describe the people, objects and the setting in the cartoon in detail. What action is taking place?

Tip: Structure your description: What do you see e. g. in the foreground, centre, background, etc.?
- Which visual elements are employed, e. g. colours (black-white contrast), which visual metaphors?
- Which (political, historical, social) events or issues may have inspired the cartoon?

Step 3: Symbolic/figurative level
Cartoonists (often) employ pictures and words to express their personal opinions.
- What tools are used to convey a certain message?
- What do the symbols used stand for?
- Which person/group does the cartoon focus on?

irony	The recognition of the difference between reality and appearance. **Verbal irony**: a contrast between what is said and what is actually meant. **Situational irony**: the opposite of what you expect to happen actually does happen.
parody	In literature, a text that imitates and slightly changes another well-known text in order to ridicule it, comment on it or trivialize it.
caricature	In literature, for example a character whose traits have been exaggerated to create a comic effect.
sarcasm	A bitter or aggressive remark used to express mockery or disapproval; often a statement which conveys the opposite of its literal meaning. In contrast to irony (gentle subtle), sarcasm is bitter and usually openly expressed.
pun	An expression involving a play on words, in which one word has two different meanings, so that a sentence can be understood in two different ways.
allusion/ reference	An allusion or reference to for example a well-known (historical) person or event, politics, popular culture, the arts or a statement from a famous work of literature.
stereo- type/ labeling	A word or phrase that describes a person in a way that is too general and often not true (*jdn. abstempeln*); cf. cliché
hyperbole	A figure of speech that contains an exaggeration.
symbol	An element of imagery in which a concrete object stands not only for itself but for some abstract idea or larger concept as well (e.g. rose → love).
visual/ pictorial metaphor	The representation of a person, thing or idea by a visual image, e.g. Uncle Sam for the United States, an elephant for India, an orange for sunshine, etc.
black humour	Humorous effects resulting rather from grotesque, morbid or macabre situations. Black humour aims to shock and disorient readers, making them laugh in the face of anxiety, suffering or death.

Step 4: Meaning and evaluation
- What is the message of the cartoon?
- Do you think the cartoon is effective in conveying its message?

Analysis of photos

To help you analyse visuals or images, here are some steps for you to follow:

Step 1: Production
- When and where was the image taken?
- Who created the image (e. g. a professional photographer, a private person, an advertising agency, etc.)?
- Was the picture arranged or was it a snapshot?
- Is the picture presented in the original version or has it e. g. been photoshopped or blue-pencilled?

Step 2: Image
- **Describe the visual elements of the image and how they are arranged.**
    - What is being shown? (e. g. surroundings, people, facial expressions, gestures, posture, clothing, accessories, etc.)
    - What are the main visual components and how are they arranged?
      Tip: In order to get a better overview of the various elements, their arrangement and relationship to each other, make a rough draft before you start to describe them.
    - Where is the viewer's eye drawn to the picture – and why? (eye-catching/visually-dominant elements)
    - What use is made of colour?
- **Explain the function and effect of visual elements and symbols.**
    - What medium is the image taken from (e. g. film, advert, photo campaign, Internet, etc.)?
    - Is the image contradictory?
    - What visual symbols are employed – and what is their function and effect?
    - State whether they imply a deeper, symbolic meaning.
    - Point out whether they appeal to the viewer/the target audience/the addressee(s).

Step 3: Addressing the audience
- **Identify and explain the message of the photo/picture.**
  - Who does the image address?
  - Is there a particular target group (e. g. a snapshot of a demonstration, etc.)?
  - What relationship is created between the image and the viewer?
  - Is more than one interpretation possible?
  - How might different viewers interpret the image and its message?
  - What emotions does the image appeal to?
  - Is there a strategy behind the image? If so, which one?
  - Are there any political/cultural/social implications?
  - Are there any historical/political/religious references?
- **State whether the visual/image/picture is effective and convincing in its message.**

visual elements:
- dancing children → motion/vitality
- a street scene → everyday life
- b/w photo → focus on contrast

visual metaphor: black and white child playing together → overcoming racism

surroundings: street in New York City

snapshot: a glimpse of reality

use of contrast: black and white

function: emotional appeal to the viewer and (indirect) political message

Helen Levitt. New York, 1940s

Characterization of a Figure in Literature

Fictional characters can be presented in a number of ways. In general, a character in a fictional text is developed through action, description, language and ways of speaking.

Types of characters

relevance within the text and characteristics	
• **protagonist** (the main character around whom most of the work revolves)	• **major characters** (main characters who dominate the story)
• **antagonist** (the person who the protagonist is against; often the villain)	• **minor characters** (less important persons who support the main character(s) by letting them interact or reveal their personalities, etc.)
• **the modern hero** (the average man/woman)	• **dynamic character** (changing and developing, with different traits)
• **the anti-hero** (often dishonest, graceless or inept person who struggles in life; the loser)	• **static characters** (unchanging, often stereotypical)
• **the tragic hero** (e.g. Macbeth; person who ends tragically as a result of personal flaws)	• **round character** (three-dimensional, with different and changing facets to the personality)
• **romantic hero** (a character with a strong will and personality who goes against established norms; often this figure experiences melancholy, isolation and unfulfilled and unhappy love)	• **flat character** (one-dimensional, viewed only from one side, often stereotypical)
• **the Hemingway hero** (a character who has been at war, drinks too much, the loner, "cowboy")	

Types of characterization in literature

- In a **direct characterization of a character** the narrator or one of the other characters **tells** the readers/audience what the character's personality is like.
- In an **indirect characterization** the writer **shows/presents** the character talking and acting which reveals the character's personality. Indirect characterization can be achieved through:
  a) **Speech** (What does the character say, how does he/she communicate and interact with others?)
  b) **Thoughts** (What is revealed through the person's private thoughts, e.g. in a monologue, soliloquy, a diary entry, etc.?)
  c) **Effect on others/on the character** (How does the person react/respond to others? Does he/she have any relationships? How do others react to the person?)
  d) **Actions** (What does the person do, how does he/she behave?)
  e) **Looks** (body language, gestures, facial expression, etc.)

How to write a literary characterization

Step 1: Collect the facts and clues given in the text and move from the outward features and characteristics to the inward nature of the character:

- **personal data** (name, age, sex, nationality)
- **outward appearance** (body, face, clothes, etc.)
- **attitudes/views** (thoughts, dreams, emotions)
- **behaviour** (toward other characters, actions)
- **relationships** (social background, family, friends)

Step 2: Draw your conclusions about the person's character and relate your findings to the text by referring to specific lines. Use the simple present for your characterization.

Step 3: Follow the introduction – main part – conclusion pattern in your characterization. Write an introductory sentence that answers the w-questions.

Mediation

Mediating a text means translating a written or recorded text from one language into another (e. g. German → English, English → German). In general, the person who is mediating must **consider the addressee(s), the meaning of the text/message, as well as cultural and situational aspects**.

When you are in a foreign country, you are constantly confronted with information/facts that you have to read or listen to: road signs, brochures, maps, (radio) announcements, advertisements, commercials, films, flight/train schedules, websites, letters, instructions, prescriptions, people talking to you, etc.

In a written examination you must consider the following aspects when asked to mediate a text:

How to mediate a text in a written examination

- **Select the most relevant information** from the text you are asked to mediate. Leave out less important details.
- **Focus** on the information **your communication partner** needs to know or what is important for the **topic**.
- Give an **analogous rendition** (*sinngemäße Wiedergabe*) of the text, not a literal translation.
- **Consider** the **addressee** (e. g. his/her cultural background).
- Take **situational aspects** into account (e. g. private, professional).
- Give **additional information** and explanations if necessary.
- **Consider** the **type of text you are required to write** (*Zieltextformat*) (e. g. a blog, a formal/informal letter, etc.).
- **Use compensation strategies** (i. e. paraphrasing, synonyms, etc.)

Criteria for evaluation

- Has the **purpose and intention** of the text been conveyed?
- Has the **addressee** been considered appropriately?
- Have the **assignments and standardized formulations** (*Operatoren*) been taken into consideration?

- Have the **characteristics of the type of text** (target text) been considered?
- Is the **formulation self-directed** (*eigenständig*) and independent?
- Do the **style and choice of words** match the intention of the text?
- Does the **construction of sentences** vary?
- Is the text **grammatically correct**?

10 tips to help mediate a written or recorded text

1. Do not translate the text word for word.
2. Listen to/watch out for keywords and the most relevant/useful/appropriate information.
3. Leave out minor details and irrelevant information (→ summarizing).
4. Try to understand the gist of the text and put it into your own words (but do not change the facts!).
5. Sometimes there are words that cannot be translated into German/English because they imply cultural differences (e.g. homecoming, gap year, cheerleading or *Schützenfest*, *Abigag*, etc.). In such cases, give examples to illustrate the situation, or add information on the cultural background if necessary.
6. Do not interpret or evaluate the text, just mediate it.
7. Express difficult passages more simply; technical terms should be replaced by everyday language.
8. Make use of paraphrases (e.g. a cheerleader is a girl who …).
9. If you do not know a word, use a synonym (= word or expression that has the same or nearly the same meaning as another in the same language).
10. If you cannot think of the right word, try simply using the opposite.

→ Beware of false friends, i.e. English words that sound or look like German ones but **differ** in meaning.

Conversation and Discussion

opening a conversation
You should always start a discussion with some kind of introductory phrase:
- I saw an interesting programme on TV last night …/I read a fascinating article in the newspaper yesterday about …/What do you think about …?
- Have you ever thought about …/What would it be like if …?
- I was really surprised to find out that …
- Did you know that …?
- Do you mind if I join you?
- Excuse me, …
- (I'm) sorry (to trouble you), but …
- Have you got time to …?

expressing your opinion/giving an opinion
- In my view, …
- In my opinion, …
- As I see it, …
- To my mind, …
- If you ask me, …
- I am sure/certain that …
- I think/believe/feel that …
- It seems to me that …
- There should be …/ought to be …
- I would like to …/I wouldn't like to …
- It would be a good idea to … (because …)

making suggestions/recommendations
- If I were you, I would …
- The best thing would be to …
- You'd better …
- Why don't you …?
- How about …?
- Have you tried/thought of … (+ gerund)?
- You should/could …

including your conversation partner
Sometimes in a discussion, you may find that you are monopolizing the conversation, and you would like to know what your partner thinks:
- So what do you think, … (+ name)?
- How do you feel about that?
- What is your view on this (matter)?
- What is your opinion about/of/on …?

interrupting your conversation partner
Sometimes it is the other way round. Your partner is monopolizing the discussion and you want to have your say:
- Can I jump in here?
- Can I just make a point?
- Perhaps I can interrupt you there.
- I'd like to get in on that if I may.
- Do you mind if I say something on that point?
- Wait a minute …
- (I'm) sorry to interrupt, but …
- Sorry, may I interrupt you for a second …
- Sorry, but did you say …?
- Can I just say/add that …
- Yes/You're right/I agree, but …
- I hope you don't mind, but …

changing the subject
These expressions help you to bring in further aspects:
- (Oh) by the way, …
- Before I forget,…
- I just thought of something …
- There's something else I wanted to ask you/say …
- Oh, now I know what I wanted to say/ask you …
- I know this has got nothing to do with what we are talking about, but …
- Could I just say … (before I forget …)
- Let's also consider …
- While I think of it, …

holding the floor
Sometimes you notice that someone is trying to interrupt you, but you haven't finished what you want to say, so you try to carry on:
- If I might just say this.
- Do you mind if I just finish what I was saying?
- I'd just like to finish making this point and then it's over to you.
- Let me just add one more thing.
- This is my final point.
- Would you please let me finish (this sentence/thought)?

returning to the original subject
Sometimes people stray from the main issue of a debate and it is necessary to get back to the topic:
- As I was saying, …
- (Now) what was I saying/what were we talking about?
- To get back to what we were talking about, …
- Let's get back to …
- (Yes, well) anyway, …
- Let's get back to the point …
- But we digress…
- Where were we before we got onto this topic?

defending yourself

If someone attacks you in a discussion, you can say:

- That's not what I said/meant at all. I was merely pointing out that …
- You've got that all wrong. What I said was …
- You're putting words in my mouth.
- You are distorting what I actually said.

expressing surprise

- I don't believe it/that!
- That's strange/funny …
- Are you (being) serious?
- Are you pulling my leg?
- Really?
- You can't mean that seriously!/You can't be serious!
- I doubt it/that/whether …
- Are you kidding me?

ending a discussion/a conversation

When you feel that you have effectively finished your discussion, that the conversation is not getting anywhere or that you have exhausted the topic, you can finish off.

- We'll just have to agree to disagree on that point.
- Further discussion is pointless, so let's end there.
- We've heard some interesting points/some new ideas, so let's stop there and go away and think about them.
- I can understand you better now, even though I don't completely agree with you.
- Well, anyway …
- Would you excuse me now, please?
- Sorry, but I've got to go now.
- I'd love to stay and discuss this further, but …
- It's been a very interesting discussion. However …
- Perhaps we can continue this another time.
- Look after yourself.
- Take care.

using fillers

- Well …
- Actually …
- You know/see …
- Let's see …
- I/you mean …
- Now let me think/see …
- In fact, …
- I wonder …
- The thing is …
- I see what you mean.
- Right then.
- Let's say …

expressing complete agreement
- You're absolutely right.
- I completely agree with you on that point.
- Precisely/Exactly.
- So do I./Me too. (agreement with a positive statement)
- Nor do I./Me neither. (agreement with a negative statement)
- That's what I think, too.

expressing partial agreement
- You're right up to a point.
- That might be the case/true.
- You could be right.
- You've got a point.
- Maybe that's true.
- That's true enough.

partial disagreement
- Do you really think so?
- Are you sure?
- That's an exaggeration.
- That's not necessarily the case/true.
- It's not as simple as that.
- I wouldn't quite say that.
- I can't imagine that.
- I find that hard to believe.

complete disagreement
Careful with this one! You do not want to make enemies, do you? Try not to be abrupt or too direct.
- That is definitely not the case.
- I'm 100 % certain of that. (disagreement with a previous negative statement)
- That's not true at all.
- You're quite wrong there.
- I totally disagree with you.

Oral Examinations

Oral exams are a lot like job interviews, so you can prepare for these in the same way that job applicants prepare – predict likely questions and practice the answers. In general, an oral exam is an opportunity for you to **demonstrate your knowledge, your presentation and speaking skills as well as your ability to communicate**. Examinations can be formal or informal, but in either case you must listen carefully to the questions and answer them directly.

The **formal exam** usually consists of a set of prepared questions and the evaluation criteria usually follow a right/wrong format. In contrast, **informal exam questions** are more open, answers are usually longer and evaluated based on problem-solving, analysis, method as well as communication and presentation skills.

Preparing for the exam

- **Collect all the material** that is likely to be covered in the exam and **try to predict essay-type questions** (i. e. questions that require a more complex answer and include a wider range of aspects. If you work with a textbook, you can use the table of contents to find possible topics.
- **Write down possible questions** on an index card. Then practice answering each possible question out loud.
- Make **a list of vocabulary terms and phrases** in connection with the possible questions.
- Then select three index cards at random (*stichprobenartig*). Pretend to be the tester and ask a question that **connects the three aspects together**. This helps you to make connections between the different topics.
- If you are a **visual learner**, you may want to draw images to boost your memory.
- **Turn off electronic equipment.**

During the exam

- Some oral exams begin with a presentation by the student. For an introduction, **give some indication of what the topic or problem is about** and why it is important.
- Give the examiner **your full attention** and look interested. Maintain **good posture** and **eye contact**.
- **Listen carefully** to the questions and make sure that you **understand exactly** what is being asked. If a short answer is requested, keep it short – if more detail is desired, give a longer response.
- Give yourself a moment to **think before you answer**. If you do not know the answer right away, feel free to take time to think. If you are able to use a blank sheet of paper and a pencil, take notes and/or draw the images you created as memory boosters.
- If you do not understand the question, **ask the examiner to reformulate, rephrase or repeat** it.
- If you cannot answer a question, **state directly that you do not know the answer** and go on.
- **Do not simply answer with "yes" or "no"**; demonstrate your knowledge by explaining aspects and backing up your answers with two or three key points or examples.
- If you are asked to describe, analyse and discuss a picture or cartoon, use the **present tense** or **present progressive** for your description. Describe the picture/cartoon **systematically** (e. g. from the foreground to the background, from right to left, etc.).
- If you need a moment to decide what to say, you can stall with formulations like "If I remember correctly", "That reminds me of …" or "If that is the case …", etc.
- If you are being evaluated together with a partner or in a group, **remember to interact with your partner(s)** and respond to his/her/their remarks. (→ FoL, Conversation and Discussion, Students' Book, pp. 385 f.).

Giving a Speech

Why giving a speech is good for you

- You learn to **speak effectively** in **different situations** and to audiences of **different backgrounds** and **levels of knowledge** and improve your **general speaking abilities**.
- The ability to speak well enough to **interest, influence or persuade people** is a major asset for your future life.
- You **gain self-confidence** by learning to overcome and manage nervousness and excitement.
- You learn **different techniques** of **using and varying your voice** and tone of speaking.
- You learn to control your **body language** and to **choose the right words** in the respective situation.
- You learn to **listen to people** to speak more effectively to them.

Non-verbal communication

The **major tools** you will use as you speak are **your voice and your body language**. Here are some aspects that help you to check yourself and be better prepared for a speech:

Voice:
- Is my voice (too) loud or (too) soft or is it monotonous?
- Do I speak (too) slowly or (too) quickly?
- Do I articulate clearly or do I mutter?
- Will my accent be a problem for my audience?
- Do I run out of air and gasp when I speak?

→ Try to **speak naturally and clearly**, and check (ask your audience) whether you can be heard.
→ **Do not shout**, because this is hard on the voice and uncomfortable for the listener.
→ Go in advance to the **room** in which you will be speaking and **familiarize yourself with its layout**.
→ **Vary your speech** (e.g. by raising and lowering your voice).

→ **Mark up your script or notes** using a highlighter on the points you want to stress.
→ **Make pauses in your talk** and give the audience and yourself time to think and reflect (e. g. use visual aids).

Body language:
- Do I rush into the room or walk in confidently and determined?
- Do I look down, hunch my shoulders and shuffle my feet (lacking confidence)?
- Do I look at the audience and smile at them before starting to speak (eye contact)?
- Do I look comfortable and businesslike?
- Do I look (too) casual or nervous?
- Do I use my hands and arms to reinforce a detail of my speech?

→ **Smile at the audience** to make them feel welcome and to **establish a good relationship**.
→ **Tell yourself that it will be a good, friendly and supportive audience** to calm yourself down.
→ **Show a cheerful**, enthusiastic **and positive state of mind**.
→ **Make eye contact** with the audience; it gives the audience the impression that you are trustworthy and honest.
→ **Put your script at the right distance** for **reading and look** up at the audience occasionally.
→ Do **not fold your arms in front of you** or put your hands in your pockets.
→ **Open your hands to show an outgoing and friendly nature** – a clenched fist indicates aggression.
→ Do not move backwards and forwards all the time while talking – you will make the audience nervous and distract them.
→ **At the end** of your speech, **leave the audience with a smile** and do not flop back in your chair with a look of exhaustion or irritation. Do not forget: The last impression will stay in the audience's mind!

Presentations

Five good reasons for giving a presentation

Just do the presentation, Williams, and let the numbers speak for themselves.

- Presentations get a discussion going.
- Presentations offer a variety of perspectives.
- Presentations provide good practice for oral examinations.
- Presentations are a good opportunity for students who can present themselves better verbally than by using written means.
- The ability to give presentations is a skill required in many occupations.

Preparing a presentation

- Have a clear focus – decide on the **key messages/information** that you want to get across.
- Be selective – identify the most relevant points.
- **Avoid overloading the audience** with everything that you know.
- Make use of the **postcard technique**:
  a) Break your presentation into sections.
  b) Give each section a heading.
  c) Write one heading and a few easily-read prompt words on each postcard.
  d) Number the postcards in the order that you want to present these points.
  → These postcards structure your talk and give you confidence.
- **Prepare audio-visual aids**, e.g. transparencies/an overhead projector, a PowerPoint, a CD and CD player, a large poster, etc. Don't overdo it, however – your talk should take centre stage and not your technical equipment.

- **Do not simply read out** what is on your transparencies or posters, etc. – paraphrase and explain them.
- **Practise your presentation** several times, going slowly and timing yourself. If your presentation is too long, edit it down. Talk slightly more slowly than in normal speech. Use a clock to time yourself.
- Provide a visual aid/handout for each person.

Giving a presentation

- Greet the audience, introduce yourself and smile at them – this creates a friendly and more relaxed atmosphere.
- Wait until everybody is quiet before you start speaking.
- Tell your audience whether you would prefer questions during the presentation or at the end.
- **Speak more slowly and loudly than usual.**
- Look up and **make eye contact** with at least two people in your audience.
- Don't apologize for anything you have not done or you feel could be better – act as though you are confident and well-prepared. This way you will win your audience's attention and confidence.
- At the beginning, briefly outline your topic by summing up what you are going to say and in which order.
- Go though your cards – pause and take a breath after each point.
- If you use difficult words or technical terms, write them on the board or on a flipchart and explain them to your audience.
- At the end, briefly sum up what you have said.
- End your presentation with a pithy (= *prägnant*) last line.
- Thank the audience for paying attention and ask them if there are any questions they want to ask.

→ Focus on Skills, Giving a Speech, Students' Book, p. 390

Continuation of a Fictional Text

Types of fictional texts you might be required to continue are
- **narrative texts** (novel, short story),
- **dramatized texts** (drama, play, one-act play),
- **film scripts** (screenplays).

Possible assignments

The assignment to continue a fictional text will usually be part of the task of working creatively with the text subsequent to the comprehension and analysis of a text. Accordingly, this task requires you to use your previous results and continue, complement or pad the text at hand with further details. You could be asked to:

- **rewrite** a scene/dialogue **from a different narrative perspective**, e.g. by choosing another or creating/adding a new character
- **rewrite** a scene/dialogue and **change the ending**, e.g. by turning the happy ending into a tragic ending or vice versa
- **elaborate on unspoken thoughts** of a character, e.g. by writing an interior monologue or a diary entry
- **continue a scene/chapter** from a (screen-)play/novel
- **change the genre of the text**, e.g. by turning a rather descriptive part in a novel into a scene in a screenplay or into dialogue with two or more characters interacting
- **change time and place** of the text and continue the scene/dialogue, etc. after a lapse of time, e.g. after 20 or more years when one of the characters has grown up, has aged and is looking back at his/her life, etc.

Your composition

Step 1: Be aware of the characteristic features of the literary genre and the type of text you are required to work with creatively. Here are some examples:

narrative texts		dramatized texts		film script
novel	**short story**	**classical drama**	**modern play**	**screenplay**
• narrator/narrative perspective • character(s) • panoramic/scenic presentation • main/subplot stream of consciousness • interior monologue • development of action/plot • disruptions/lapses in time/foreshadowing/flashback, etc. • spoken/everyday English, informal English	• immediate beginning • open ending • exceptional incident in everyday life • spoken English	• protagonist/antagonist/hero • dialogue/monologue/soliloquy • stage directions • acts/scenes • spoken English • development of a conflict • often linear development • happy/tragic ending/resolution	• everyday character(s) • internal conflict • current topics, e.g. society, politics, crisis, war, etc. • stage directions • disruptions/lapses in time • spoken English	• slug lines • dialogue/monologue • action • focus on visual aspects • technical directions (props, music, camera operations) • spoken English

Step 2: Employ the above-mentioned **formal characteristics of the respective genre** in your text.

Step 3: The **stage directions** require you to briefly characterize the speaker's intentions, emotions or behaviour. In order to avoid overusing verbs like "think", "say" or "give", use a dictionary to find alternative formulations, e. g. to reflect, to consider, etc.

Step 4: Make the characters interact and not just deliver monologues. They can use questions or interrupt each other, etc.

Writing a Comment and a Review

A Comment

A written comment expresses your personal opinion on a certain topic or issue. It is a common means used in print media in order to state one's opinion to the readership in a more or less critical way. Take some notes first, and structure your thoughts systematically before starting to write.

1. Introduction
- Make some introductory remarks in which you, for example, raise a question, refer to a current problem, etc.
- The introduction should clarify your topic/concern.

2. Main part – arguments
- State, demonstrate and describe the positive and negative effects of a topic/situation.
- Support your view of the situation by giving examples. You can, for example, refer to or quote famous people or experts on this matter, or relate it to other comparable issues.
- Emphasize the argument by referring to further/future consequences.

3. Conclusion
- Conclude your comment by giving your personal view of the situation/problem.
- Strategically, it is smart to relate your final remarks to your introduction in order to finally "wrap up" the topic and make your point.
- → Focus on Language, Conversation and Discussion, Students' Book, pp. 385 f.

A Review of a Fiction Book or Film

Step 1: Plot*/characters*/theme*
- Briefly summarize the plot of the book/film (approx. 150 words). ("Who/where/when/what/why"-questions should be answered.)

- Include the type of film (e. g. feature film*, western)/ book (e. g. historical novel), title, author/director, publishing/release year, edition, special features.
- Briefly describe the main characters* and how they are related.
- Briefly outline the basic theme(s) and leitmotif(s)* of the book/film.
- Describe the overall atmosphere.

Step 2: Narrative/cinematic aspects
- Point out striking narrative qualities (e. g. point of view*, metaphorical language, structure of the plot*).
- Refer to any striking cinematic devices that create/reinforce the atmosphere of the film.
- Mention which actors were chosen for the respective roles.
- Explain what the book's/film's message and the author's/director's intention may be.

Step 3: Evaluation
- Say what you like or dislike about: the plot, structure, directing, camera work, sound, special effects, casting and performance of the actors.
- Explain whether the book/film has successfully conveyed any/its main message.
- Comment on the actors: Have they successfully personified and typified the characters?
- Consider and quantify shortcomings/weaknesses and strengths of the book/film.
- If the film is a literary adaptation: How well has the story been adapted? – Is there anything missing (in comparison to the novel)? – or in comparison to other books/films by the same author/director?

Step 4: Conclusion
- Is the film worth viewing?/Is the book worth reading?
- Would you recommend the book/film? – What was your favourite part of the book/film?

Writing an Analysis

Writing a text analysis usually follows a standardized pattern, regardless of what kind of text or material you are required to analyse, e.g. a fictional or non-fictional text, a political speech, an excerpt from a play or a cartoon.

General aspects

Before writing:

- **Read the assignment carefully** and make sure that you have understood what exactly you are required to do. Pay particular attention to the **standardized terminology** (*Operatoren*) which tell you what to focus on.
- Pay attention to **additional keywords** given in the assignment, e.g. which (stylistic) aspects of the text or which features of a character you are expected to analyse in particular.
- Read the text as often as necessary to **understand it thoroughly**. Underline and/or highlight the parts that are significant and important with regard to the assignment. Note down your observations and make notes in the margin of the text. Use your dictionary to crosscheck that you have understood expressions and formulations in the text correctly.
- Find the **main issue or message** that the text addresses and the **writer's position** in this regard.

While writing:

- Check for **features/references to lines to support your findings**, e.g. arguments, line of argument, choice of words, facts and numbers given, quotes from further experts, etc.
- Prepare a **draft outline** (*Entwurf, Konzeption*) of the text you want to write. Do not write every single sentence line-by-line but take notes on **a)** how you want to structure your composition, **b)** which textual references and quotes you want to use and **c)** what background knowledge you want to use and refer to.

- Pay attention to details: do not cover everything but focus on the most relevant/striking aspects.
- **Avoid wordy and generalized explanations** and repetitions but be **specific and precise**.
- Do not include your personal opinion or beliefs on the matter but be **factual and neutral**.

After writing:
- **Proofread** your analysis and crosscheck that you have not forgotten anything from your draft outline. Check for grammatical correctness, punctuation, spelling and that your composition is written in the **present tense**.

Your composition

Introduction
- Formulate a **connecting sentence at the beginning** in which you refer to a relevant aspect from your comprehension. Briefly state that the writer for example uses a specific line of argument to underline his ideas.
  Example: *As I have pointed out in the first part of my composition, the writer XY aims at persuading the reader of his critical view of the USA. In order to emphasize his position he uses several persuasive techniques which will be explained in the following.*
- Give a **concise** (*kurzgefasst*) **outline of the structure** of the text, referring to the writer's train of thought and/or line of argument and the general message of the text.
- **Do not repeat** the introductory part from your first assignment (w-questions).

Main part
- Use the **three-step method** for your analysis:

Step 1: Quote from the text	Step 2: Use the correct technical term	Step 3: Explain the function
(ll. #) "… some citizens, many people, the whole world …"	→ climax, parallelism	→ emphasis on numbers and amounts involved

- Do not just follow the chronological order of the text but also **focus on relevant aspects, stylistic devices, characters**.
- Be careful to **quote correctly**.

Conclusion
- End your text by **referring to your introduction** and formulating a **concluding sentence** in which you for example refer to the message or the type of the text (again).
- **Do not evaluate** the text. Stay factual and concise.

A newspaper commentary/an editorial

In contrast to a newspaper report, **a commentary or an editorial presents the newspaper's opinion on an issue**. Editorial writers build on an argument and try to influence the reader's opinion, **criticize** a certain issue or try to **clarify a complicated or controversial** matter. Sometimes they ask people to take action. In a nutshell, editorials are **opinionated news stories** which are **personalized** and which **evaluate** issues or events.

Structure
- **headline**
- **introduction, body, paragraphs, conclusion**
- **an objective explanation of the issue**
- **opinions from the opposing viewpoint**
- **opinions of the writer**
- **alternative solutions to the problem or issue being criticized**
- **a solid and concise conclusion**

How to write a newspaper commentary/an editorial

Step 1: Choose a significant topic that would interest readers.

Step 2: Do research/collect information, facts, statistical data, etc.

Step 3: In an introduction, state your opinion briefly, e. g. *Have you ever thought about …? Taking into account that … Looking at the latest results of … one should … I think that …*

Step 4: Explain the topic/issue objectively and explain why this topic is important, e. g. *Looking at the facts/numbers we do have to realize that … therefore it is our responsibility to …*

Step 5: Give the opposing viewpoint first with its quotations and facts, e. g. *On the contrary one might think that … the numbers suggest that … on the surface the situation appears to be …*

Step 6: Refute the opposing viewpoint and develop your case:
- present at least three arguments
- the strongest argument should come last
- back up your arguments by facts, e. g. statistics, quotations, expert information, etc.
- if you comment on a text, refer to the text with quotes to substantiate your arguments

Step 7: Repeat key phrases to reinforce an idea, e. g. *Let us get back to … Let us take a closer look at … This situation requires a clear judgment … We have no option but to …*

Step 8: Employ rhetorical devices to make your article more convincing (e. g. comparison, antithesis, metaphorical expressions).

Step 9: Give a (realistic) solution to the problem and encourage constructive criticism and pro-active reaction.

Step 10: Sum up the information and recapture important points and solutions. Refer back to your introductory remarks and statement. Your conclusion should have some punch, e. g. *If we do not take action against dangerous and poisonous food, who will?*

Writing a Formal Letter

Business letter/letter of complaint – layout

1. letterhead with postcode, telephone and fax numbers and e-mail
2. reference initials
3. date
4. inside address, including street, ZIP code, country
5. attention line
6. salutation
   - *Dear Sir or Madam* → used if name is unknown
   - *Miss* → unmarried woman (old use)
   - *Mrs* → married woman
   - *Ms* → unclear if the woman is married or not
   - *Mr* → man
   - no comma at the end of the salutation
7. subject line (optional)
   - after salutation in the UK
   - before salutation in the USA
   - in bold type
   - capitalized
8. body of the letter
   - begin with a capital letter
   - paragraphs are separated by a free line
9. complimentary close
   - *Yours sincerely* → most common use
   - *Yours faithfully* → formal, only used if the name of the addressee is unknown
   - *(Best) Regards, Best wishes* → friendly
   - signature, name, position of the signatory
10. enclosure (*Anlage*)
    - Enc (singular), e.g. *order form*
    - Encs (plural), e.g. *cheque, folder*

Basic types of business letters

- **Enquiry:** a request for or question about information about sth. (*Anfrage*)
- **Offer:** a voluntary but conditional promise given by a buyer or seller to another for acceptance (*Angebot*)
- **Order:** a request to make or supply goods (*Bestellung*)
- **Reminder:** a request for an overdue payment that should have been paid by an earlier date (*Mahnung*)
- **Letter of complaint:** a request to deal with and solve a problem, e.g. delay in delivery, unsatisfactory or defective goods, wrong goods, etc. (*Beschwerdebrief, Reklamation*)

Tel: +49(0)221 123456
Fax: +49(0)221 1234567
tobymueller@web.de

① Gartenweg 20
54327 Köln
Germany

③ 15 May 2016

② **Your ref: TBS/1234**

④ Digital World Inc.
8607 Main Street
Cornerstone, NJ 23657
USA

⑤ Attention: Ms Goldwell, Customer Services

⑥ Dear Ms Goldwell

⑦ **My Order No. CF-23405 – Smartphone "Stay Connected", black, dated 4 March 2016**

⑧ The above-mentioned smartphone was delivered to me today and on opening the package I found that
- the touchscreen is badly scratched
- the GPS navigation does not work properly
- applications cannot be downloaded
- the headset is missing

Obviously the smartphone was poorly packed and roughly handled in transit and something must have gone wrong in production and while packaging the phone.

Needless to say, I cannot use the phone and thus would like to return it at your expense.

I am looking forward to hearing what you have to say about the matter and would welcome an immediate replacement of the damaged article.

⑨ Yours sincerely

Tobias Müller
Tobias Müller

⑩ Enc.: Copy of the packaging slip and invoice

Writing an Interview

In a written examination you might be required to **write an interview as a creative writing task** in addition to the comprehension and the analysis tasks. Your written interview text should be written in such a way that it can serve as a script or draft (*Vorlage*) for an interview you are asked to conduct. In general, an interview is a conversation between two (or more) people, (an) **interviewer(s)** and an **interviewee**, where (usually pre-formulated) questions are asked by the interviewer(s) to obtain information, facts or statements on a certain topic. In journalism, interviews are used to collect information, or present views and assessments to viewers or listeners. Interviews are also important in qualitative research, e. g. when interviewing an expert in some field.

Types of interviews

- **informal, conversational interview**
  No pre-formulated questions are asked; the interviewer stays as open and adaptable to the interviewee's nature, response and priorities as possible.
- **general interview**
  The focus is on collecting more general information from the interviewee; the interviewer pre-formulates questions but stays open to the interviewee's focus and priorities on a certain matter.
- **standardized, open-ended interview**
  The same, standardized and pre-formulated questions are asked to different interviewees. This method allows for rather fast interviews that can be easily analysed and compared.
- **closed, fixed response interview**
  All interviewees are asked the same pre-formulated questions and are asked to choose questions from the same set of alternatives.

The interviewer

Although the general aim of an interview is to elicit (*hervorlocken*) information from an interviewee by strategically and skilfully posing questions, the interviewer should follow certain rules. He/She should be **neutral**, **unemotional** and **unbiased**.

Technique and structure

- **introduction of the topic**; the reason for the interview/the occasion; introduction of the **interviewee(s)**, their background, position and reason for being interviewed on the matter, e.g. *Good evening … today our topic is … I would like to welcome our special guest … who is an expert in …*
- asking a **well-structured** sequence of (pre-formulated) questions
- **listening and reacting** to the interviewee(s) in order to achieve more focus and attention to detail
- asking **follow-up questions** throughout the interview to
  a) enable the interviewee to elaborate on certain topics and to gain more comprehensive information
  b) to clarify complicated or confusing aspects, e.g. *What do you mean by saying …? Could you elaborate on … and give us some more details on …?*
- asking **precise and respectful questions** in order not to offend the interviewee or make him/her become defensive or unwilling to share
- making the interviewee(s) feel comfortable and respected by **avoiding interrupting** him/them whenever possible
- **ending the interview** by
  a) summarizing the result of the discussion or the views taken by the participants
  b) thanking the participants, e.g. *I am sorry to say that our time is up. Thank you, … it has been most comprehensive … informative … It has been a pleasure to have you with us.*
- using **spoken English** (not formal, but avoiding colloquial English or slang)

Writing a Newspaper Article

In general, newspaper reports aim **at informing their readership** about events that have happened in their local area, or about national and international news. Newspaper reports usually **provide answers** to questions (who, what, where, when, why, how). They should be **easy to read, objective and present reliable, unbiased facts and information** and should be written in a snappy and concise style. However, the style of an article and the language register (formal, informal) depends on the type of newspaper the article is published in, e.g. a quality paper, a popular paper, etc.

Types of newspaper articles

- **local news** (focussing on the neighbourhood/the region)
- **national news** (focussing on one's country)
- **international news** (world news)
- **a feature article** ("soft news", e.g. about a celebrity; a person who does volunteer work in the community; a movie review, etc.; it is **not** considered a news story)
- **editorial** (an article that contains the writer's, publisher's or editor's opinion on an issue)
- **a column** (an article written by the same person on a regular basis, about subjects of interest to him/her, current events or community happenings; it is not considered a news story)

General structure/layout

- **headline** (catching the reader's attention)
- **sub-headlines** (structuring the article)
- **columns/paragraphs** (structuring the article; all paragraphs relate to the main idea/topic)
- **pictures, photos, graphics, visuals,** etc. (illustration, proof)
- **first paragraph** (introduces the main point of the story (who?); introduces the main idea (what?))

- **following paragraphs** (provide answers to the other questions (where, when, why, how); develop the main idea)
- **paragraphs** (short, punchy, not too long)
- **information** (clear, concise, factual)
- **language** (precise, clear sentence structure, explanation of technical terms)
- **grammatical tense** (usually past tense – when an event has already taken place)
- **references** to
   a) what people said (quotations/direct speech; reported speech),
   b) sources, further/former articles on the topic, etc.

How to write a newspaper report

Step 1: Select your target group (e.g. students, readers in a small town, a neighbourhood, etc.).

Step 2: Find a subject of interest (e.g. the expenses of schoolbooks or field trips; the quality of clothes, etc.).

Step 3: Do research on the matter (e.g. interviewing people, Internet research, etc.).

Step 4: List your potential sources. They shoud be reliable/credible (e.g. authority, expert, hero, witness, ordinary people, etc.).

Step 5: Write your lead-in (the introductory paragraph).

Step 6: Write the rest of your article and
- structure it into paragraphs of 4–5 lines,
- develop a clear train of thought and line of argument,
- employ references to prove the reliability of your information.

Step 7: Find a suitable title for your report. It should be vivid and catchy and announce the topic in a short and concise way. Try to evoke your reader's interest by asking a question (*Why is ethical fashion so expensive?*) or using an exclamation mark (*No Boring Lessons Any Longer!*).

Note: The information given in a newspaper article should be true, objective and original.

Writing a Speech Script

In your written examination, you might be asked to write a speech in response to a text you analysed or on an issue related to the text at hand. A good speech always has a clear and distinct structure and follows clear-cut lines of argumentation and trains of thought.

Structure

Introduction

In order to **win your audience's attention** and **attract their interest** you can start by
- saying sth. thought-provoking,
- telling a joke,
- saying sth. controversial,
- citing an interesting quotation.

After having gained their attention, you should **introduce yourself** and **the subject** you are going to talk about.

Additionally, you can make a positive remark/pay a compliment to the place where you are speaking, the audience, etc. – this will help you to bond with your audience.

Tips on vocab

> Good evening, ladies and gentlemen. ■ Dear friends … ■ I feel deeply honoured to speak to such an illustrious audience. ■ Let me thank you for inviting me to this impressive meeting. ■ It is a great pleasure to be here and to talk to you. ■ As … said, it is never too late to take action. ■ Wouldn't it be wonderful if we managed to … ■ Let me assure you …

Main part/body of the speech

This is the longest part of your speech and should therefore have a clear structure, following a topical order, a line of argumentation or a train of thought.

- Start with a **thought-provoking**, **important thought** or argument.
- Decide on which pattern you want to choose for the **body of your speech**:

a) **progressive structure** (developing on a cause-to-effect or problem-solution arrangement)
   → effect: clarity, unity and logical coherence
b) **antithetical structure** (contrasting and juxtaposing of facts, ideas, arguments)
   → effect: clarity and emphasis through comparison and contrast

- **Support your arguments** with
  a) information (e.g. statistical data, facts),
  b) examples,
  c) quotations (e.g. of experts, political authorities, etc.),
  d) references to similar situations.
- **Work in some rhetorical devices**, e.g. alliterations, repetitions of relevant phrases/words/numbers, contrast, comparison, climax, rhetorical questions.
- **Use linkers and connectives** to vary the beginning of your sentences and to connect your thoughts and arguments.

Conclusion

This part of your speech is very important because it gives you the opportunity to end with a punch and/or an appeal that will stay in your audience's mind.

- Give a **concise summary of the most relevant points** of your speech.
- Finish with a **punchy remark, a call for action** or sth. personal to **reinforce your line of argument**.
- Relate your finishing remarks to the beginning of your speech in order to **round off your speech**.

Tips on vocab

> Let me quote … again, … ■ (to put it) in a nutshell … ■ to put it bluntly … ■ Let us be honest, shouldn't we … ■ Now that you have realized the importance of … ■ I put my trust in you to … ■ I have absolutely no doubt that you will make the right decision. ■ Let us roll up our sleeves and get to work.

Writing a Summary

A **summary or an abstract** (*Zusammenfassung, Inhaltsangabe*) is common in all forms of writing and is aimed at **highlighting the major points** of a piece of writing and outlining the most important facts. Furthermore, it helps you to obtain a better **orientation and understanding of the structure and contents of a text** which you need for additional analysis and evaluation.

General aspects

A summary ...
- gives the **most relevant facts** and the overall meaning of a text,
- must not contain your own thoughts and opinions,
- begins with an **introductory sentence**,
- is about 150–200 words long, depending on the length of the text that is to be summed up,
- **must not contain direct speech or quotations**,
- should be **factual**,
- leaves out irrelevant details,
- should usually be written in the **present tense**,
- should present the events in **chronological order** (→ no suspense),
- closes with a sentence that **sums up the main message of the text and its intention**,
- prepares the analysis part of your composition – it must not analyse the text but **strictly focuses on depicting** *(wiedergeben)* **the text** in your own words.

Your composition

Before writing:
- **Underline** the most relevant aspects and facts given in the text.
- **Divide the text into paragraphs**/thematic units and **find a suitable headline** for each paragraph.

- Make sure that you understand everything – if necessary, **cross-check the meaning of words** or expressions in your dictionary.
- Do not underline every detail but focus on the **most important information/striking keywords**.

While writing:
- **Use the present tense** for your text.
- Write an **introductory sentence** which answers the **w-questions** and informs about the **source** of the text: author, title of the text, type of text, topic, place and year of publication, information about whether the text is an excerpt or was abbreviated.
- Do not copy the words and expressions used in the text but **use your own words and/or try to find synonyms to paraphrase** the main aspects. Use your dictionary to find alternative formulations.
- **Do not quote** from the text and **do not use direct speech** (!).
- **Do not refer to any specific lines** in the text.
- **Use formulations** to state what the text/author writes about or wants to express.
  Example: *The author makes remarks on…; The author expresses his/her concerns about …*
- Be careful to not just follow the chronology of the text, but **restructure it and focus on key aspects/focal points** (*Schwerpunkte*).
- **Do not use short forms**.
- **Use standard English** for your summary even though the text you are to summarize may be written in informal English or in verse, etc.

After writing:
- **Proofread your text** and check for grammatical correctness, punctuation and spelling. Make sure that you have used the **present tense**.

Writing a Letter to the Editor

A letter to the editor is a **formal letter** that has **different functions**:

A reader …

… **responds to an article** in a newspaper/magazine/on the Internet he/she has read and **states his/her opinion on the matter**.

… **expresses his/her criticism or support** of a stance taken by the publication.

… responds to **another reader's letter** to the editor.

… **comments on a current issue** or a problem of public interest.

… **remarks on materials** that have appeared in a (previous) publication.

… **corrects** a perceived **error or misinterpretation**.

Tips for writing

- **Read the publication thoroughly** and underline/highlight key phrases and the most relevant parts.
- Pay attention to the **focus and the standardized terminology** used in **your assignment**, e.g. *Write a letter to the editor and assess the author's view of immigration to Great Britain*.
- **Name the article** you are responding to in the first sentence of the body of your letter or in a subject line.
- Include your **name, address and e-mail address (phone number)** at the top of your letter to give the editor the opportunity to verify your identity.
- Since your letter may be edited, **get to the point and be concise** (*knapp und präzise*) and focused. Do not write a lengthy argument.
- Limit your letter to **two or three paragraphs**:
  a) **Introduce** the subject matter and briefly state your opinion/objection (*Einwand*).

b) Include a few sentences (**arguments, examples**) to support your view.
c) End with a **concluding remark** and a clever, punchy (*ausdrucksstark*) line.

Keep in mind that a letter to the editor is a formal letter. Use **Standard English** and write in **a matter-of-fact style**, using clearly structured arguments. Avoid informal and insulting (*beleidigend*) or offensive language and do not be overly emotional.

Start your letter like this:
Dear Editor/Sir/Madam,
I am writing in response to the article …

- **If you do not want your name published**, state so clearly, e. g. in the last paragraph.
- Example: *"Please note, I do not want my (full) name published with this letter".*
- **Proofread** your letter to check for poor grammar and spelling errors.
- **Submit** your letter by e-mail (if possible) to enable the editor to cut and paste your letter.

Tips on vocab

to have a good/positive opinion about sb./sth. ■ to (strongly) (dis-)agree with sb. about sth. ■ to approve of sb./sth. (*billigen*) ■ to advise sb. to do sth. (*raten, beraten*) ■ to acknowledge that … (*anerkennen*) ■ to show one's solidarity with … ■ to argue in support of sb./sth. (*sich aussprechen für …*) ■ to take a negative view of sb./sth. ■ to refute sb.'s arguments (*entkräften, widerlegen*) ■ to express criticism of … ■ to call sth. into question ■ to express doubts about sb./sth. (*jdn./etw. anzweifeln*) ■ to protest against ■ to have reservations about (*Vorbehalte haben*) ■ to disassociate oneself from sb./sth. (*sich distanzieren von*) ■ to make remarks on ■ to make observations about ■ to maintain/claim that … (*behaupten*)

Connectives and Adverbs

In order to improve your style and speak and write more fluently, you should employ connectives and adverbs. **Try to vary the beginnings of your sentences** and use sub-clauses to express your opinion and thoughts in a more diversified way.

listing/order first, second, third; firstly, secondly, thirdly; for one thing ... (and) for another (thing); to begin with; to start with; initially/in the first place; then; finally; to conclude[1]; last but not least	**adding/reinforcing**[11] also; as well; too; furthermore; moreover; then; in addition to; above all; what is more; again; equally; generally speaking
comparison/similarity[2] equally; likewise; similarly; in the same way; compared to ...; both; but while the first ...; although; though	**summary/conclusion/consequence** then; all in all; to sum up; in conclusion; accordingly; as a result; briefly; consequently; generally speaking; hence; it follows that; taking everything into account; thus; therefore
exemplification[3] namely; for example (e.g.); for instance; that is (i.e.); that is to say	**reformulation** or rather; to put it another way; in other words
alternative alternatively; on the other hand	**contrast** on the contrary; in contrast; by contrast; on the one hand ... on the other hand; compared to; although; likewise
concession[4] besides; however; nevertheless; still; though; in spite of that; on the other hand; despite this; admittedly[5]	**reason and purpose** as; because of; consequently; for this/that reason; hence; in order to; on account of; since; so; that explains why; this is why; therefore

emphasis[6] as a matter of fact; at any rate; clearly; evidently[7]; ideally; undoubtedly[8]	**condition** as long as; even if; if; in any case; on the condition that; provided that; unless
your own opinion from my point of view; in my opinion; in my view; the way I see it; to my mind; to my way of thinking	**an opposite point of view** alternatively; but; despite/in spite of (the fact); except for; however; in contrast to; instead of; nonetheless; on the contrary
reference[9] **to something/ someone** according to; as for; the former; the latter; with reference to; referring to; with regard to; concerning	**assumption**[12] assuming that; given that; presumably; probably; granted that; allegedly[13]; seemingly; on the face of it; supposedly[14]
toning down[10] **arguments** a little (worrying); almost; fairly; hardly; more or less; somewhat; on second thought; at first sight	**emphasizing arguments** actually; absolutely; (not …) at all; badly (needed); completely; extremely; entirely; indeed; not in the least; perfectly; really; seriously; thoroughly; totally; utterly[15]; very

---

[1] **to conclude sth. from sth.** *schlussfolgern* – [2] **similarity** the state of being like sth./sb. but not exactly the same – [3] **exemplification** illustration, giving an example – [4] **concession** *Zugeständnis* – [5] **admittedly** accepting that sth. is true – [6] **to put emphasis on sth.** to stress sth. – [7] **evidently** clearly, obviously – [8] **undoubtedly** *zweifellos* – [9] **reference** sth. that you connect or relate to sth. else – [10] **to tone down sth.** to express an opinion in a less extreme or offensive way – [11] **to reinforce sth.** to make a feeling/an idea stronger – [12] **assumption** *Annahme, Vermutung* – [13] **allegedly** *angeblich* – [14] **supposedly** *angeblich, vermutlich* – [15] **utterly** totally, very much

Vocabulary and Phrases for Text Analysis

When you are asked to analyse and interpret a text, you should express yourself precisely and appropriately. Therefore, it is important to use a specific terminology that employs technical terms (e. g. stylistic devices) and a variety of formulations that make your text more fluent and less repetitive.

The following words and phrases are related to the most relevant aspects.

introduction	the author
• The text deals with/is about … • The theme of the text is … • The text is composed of/consists of … • Three/two … different parts can be distinguished … • The first part runs from line … to line … • At the beginning of the text, … • The author begins by saying … • At the end of the text,/Finally,/Lastly, … • The first part forms the introduction … • The main/central/principal idea is … • In the conclusion, the author states that … • In the final part, the author …	• The author thinks/says/believes that … • According to the author, …/In his/her view … • The author illustrates his/her point of view with … • The author makes a comment on … • The author is convinced that … • The author's judgements are (un)realistic/not objective/unfounded/well-founded … • The reader can sympathize with the author's view on … • The author expresses doubts/questions … • The author makes remarks on … • The intention/aim/objective of the author is … • The author portrays believable characters. • The author gives a detailed/vague description of …

the text/the plot/the story

- The story is told from the perspective of …
- The plot is set in …
- The text is written in an ironic tone.
- The text contains comical elements.
- The setting of the action is unreal/imaginary.
- The action becomes more/less intense …
- The situation seems quite absurd…
- Suspense is created because/by …
- The ending of the story is believable …

the characters

- The main/principal character in the story is …
- The author characterizes him/her as …
- He has many positive traits …
- His behaviour is marked by …
- Another essential quality is …
- She shows her superiority by saying that …
- He is characterized as …
- The protagonist lacks …
- As far as his outward appearance is concerned, …
- She plays an important/a secondary role …

the structure

- The exposition gives information about …
- The first scene introduces …
- The starting point for the action is …
- The conflict reaches its climax in …
- The turning point is indicated by …
- The crisis is in scene …
- In the last scene, …
- This play/story has a happy/tragic ending.

the action

- The action takes place in …
- The action develops in … stages …
- The action progresses fast …
- The scene contains a flashback.
- The action is interrupted by …
- This is one of the central scenes …
- The development of the action is slowed down by …

Focus on Language

purpose (of texts)

- The author wants to arouse the reader's interest.
- The text appeals to …
- He tries to manipulate …
- He/She wants the reader to become aware of …
- The text addresses young/poor/… people …
- It is the author's objective to create a feeling of …
- The author attempts to influence the reader by …
- The advert suggests to the reader that …

vocabulary

- The vocabulary contains many colloquial expressions/technical terms …
- This word/term expresses fear …
- This word has a negative meaning/negative associations …
- This phrase suggests …
- These phrases belong to the spoken language.
- The choice of words gives the text its romantic/technical/… character.
- These expressions are typical of …

criticizing the author

- I (dis-)agree with the author on …
- I do not understand why he/she …
- I consider it to be wrong/difficult to …
- This … cannot be taken seriously …
- I would like to comment on …
- It must be pointed out that …
- This statement contradicts his view of …
- There is a contradiction in …
- It goes without saying that …
- It is essential that …
- This raises the question as to why he/she …
- What really matters is …
- This problem has nothing to do with …
- This is of no importance/significance for …

further useful expressions

- To give an explanation for …
- The author pretends to know …
- The author describes the characteristics of …
- The article is based on …
- The author makes an allusion to …
- This sentence reveals the true character of …
- He/She appeals to emotions rather than …
- He/She quotes some experts as an example of …
- The article relates … to …
- The text conveys the impression that …
- The writer establishes a relationship between …
- The author's theses are …
- He supports his thesis with …
- Her outlook on life is …

- As far as ... is concerned, ...
- From this point of view, ...
- Generally speaking, ...
- As a matter of fact, ...
- In theory, ..., but in reality, ...

- He/She takes a positive/negative view of ...
- The author generalizes about ...
- This is a great simplification of ...

→ When you analyse or interpret a text, you should use **Standard English**.

→ You should generally use the **present tense** when you describe/explain or analyse specific aspects of the text.

→ Be careful not to imitate the tone or the language of the text – when you write about a text written in colloquial English, you still should use Standard English in order to appear **impersonal and objective**.

→ Try to **vary the beginnings of your sentences** by employing different connectives.

→ Even when you express your personal opinion about a text/the author, etc., your choice of words should be appropriate and respectful. It can be helpful *not* to begin sentences with "I ..." or "I think ..." but to **focus on the text, the author**, etc. (e.g. *The article gives the impression that ..., The author seems to intend to ...*). This appears much more impersonal and academic.

→ **Do not overdo it by being too formal** or stilted – your text should reflect your view and stance on the matter.

→ Be careful **not to use short forms** (e.g. don't, doesn't, there's, haven't, you're, etc.) in the tasks that are related to the **comprehension, analysis and comment/evaluation** of texts. They should only be used in creative writing tasks, e.g. in an informal conversation, diary entry, or interior monologue, when you are asked to express your thoughts in a rather informal way. However, when you write e.g. a letter to the editor, you should use formal English.

Note: Explanations of the respective technical terms can be found in the Literary Terms section, Studtens' Book, pp. 405 ff.

A

abbreviations (scripts) 111
administration 23
adverbs 158 f.
Africa 88 ff.
American Dream 76
analysis 100 ff.
– fictional text 100 f.
– film scene 108 f.
– non-fictional text 102 f.
– poetry/lyrics 114 f.
– political speech 116 f.
– statistical data 118 f.
– visuals 120 ff.
– screenplay 110 f.
application 146

B

beliefs/values 25 ff., 76
biotechnology 96
Black Power 78 ff.
Britain's global role 58 ff.
British Empire 10 ff., 58 f.
business 146 f.

C

cartoon 120 ff.
challenges for a modern India 72 f.
characterization 124 f.
checks & balances 84
civil rights movement 78 ff.
colonization 12 ff., 58 ff.
comment/review 140 f.
commercial correspondence
– business letter 146 ff.
– order 146 ff.
Commonwealth 6 f., 62 f.
Commonwealth of Nations 62 f.
communication 47 f., 51 f., 58 ff., 98.
connectives 158 f.
constitution/independence/treaties 9 f.
consumerism/consumption 34 f.
continuation of a fictional text 138 f.
conversation (vocab/phrases) 128 ff.
crisis/war/poverty 31 ff.
civil rights/freedom/equality 78 ff.

D

decolonization 88 ff.
democracy 42 ff.
discussion (vocab/phrases) 128 ff.

E

ecology/energy 40 ff.
economy/trade 18 ff., 29 ff., 34 ff, 90 f., 92 f.
elections (voting) 70 f., 84 f.
electoral system 70 f., 84 f.
emancipation (slaves) 78 ff.

Empire, the 58 ff.
Englishes 47 ff.
environment 40 f.
equal rights/equality 78 ff.
European Union 68 f.
examination (oral) 135 f.
executive 70 ff., 84 ff.

F
formal letter 146 f.

G
G8 93
G20 93
genetic engineering 96 f.
globalization/global economy 34 ff., 38 ff., 90 f.
Great Britain 64 ff.

H
historical development 15 f.
history (British Empire) 53 ff.
history (India) 72 ff.
history (US) 21 ff.
House of Commons 70 f.
House of Lords 70 f.

I
immigration/minorities 28 f., 64 ff., 82 ff.
Industrial Revolution 58, 90
imperialism 58 ff., 88 ff.
Inaugural address 84 ff.

India/Indian independence 16 ff., 72 ff.
interview 148 f.

J
(online) journalism 55 f.
judiciary 70 ff., 84 ff.

L
labour policy 36 ff.
language 47 ff.
legislative 70 ff., 84 ff.
letter to the editor 156 f.

M
(mass) (social) media (also electronic/digital) 51 f., 53 ff.
mediation 126 f.
melting pot 76 f.
migration (see immigration)
minorities 64 ff., 82 ff.
monarchy 70 ff.
multicultural Britain 7 ff.

N
newspaper article 150 f.

P
parliament 70 ff.
patriotism 77 f.
photo 120 ff.
Pilgrim Fathers 21 f.
poetry 114 f.

political speech 116 f.
political systems 44 ff.
- UK 70 ff.
- US 84 ff.
politics/constitution 23 f.
presentation 136 f.
President 84 ff.
press 112 f.
Prime Minister 70 ff.
puritanism/protestant work ethic 76 ff.
Pursuit of Happiness 76 ff.

R
Raj, the 72 ff.
review 140 f.
(fundamental, inalienable and God-given) rights 76 ff.

S
science and technology 45 ff., 96 f.
screenplay 110 f.
segregation 78 ff.
separation/sharing of powers 70 ff., 84 ff.
slavery 58 ff., 78 ff.
society/values 45 f., 118 f.
(open and dynamic) society 76 ff.

song (lyrics) 114 f.
speech (giving) 134 f.
speech script 152 f.
summary 154 f.

T
technology 45 f.
text analysis (vocab/phrases) 160 ff.
texts (basic types)
- fictional text 100 f.
- non-fictional text 102 f.
- complex texts 104 f.
trade 34 ff., 92 f.
trade unions/labour policy 36 ff.
(system of) triangle trading 58 f.

U
United Nations 94 ff.
USA 76 ff., 82 ff.

W
working 36 f.
world trade 92 ff.
World Economic Forum 92 ff.

Picture acknowledgements

|alamy images, Abingdon/Oxfordshire: Barritt, Peter 60; Granger Historical Picture Archive 77; grzegorz knec 86, 86, 92; White, Jonny 70, 70. |Art Explosion, Calabasas, CA: 72, 82, 140, 141. |Berghahn, Matthias, Bielefeld: 140, 156. |CartoonStock.com, Bath: 110; Ralph Hagen 136. |Domke, Franz-Josef, Hannover: 58, 61, 62, 64, 65, 66, 67, 69, 71, 75, 84, 89, 94, 96, 118, 119, 119. |Edelbrock, Iris, Viersen: 76. |Focus Photo- u. Presseagentur GmbH, Hamburg: elliott erwitt/Magnum Photos 78. |Fotofinder GmbH, Berlin: The Art Archive 72. |fotolia.com, New York: jpegwiz 134; niroworld 99; Pixel Embargo 154. |Getty Images, München: Bettmann/CORBIS 81. |Kassing, Reinhild, Kassel: 116, 142. |Laux, Hans-Dieter, Bonn / Thieme, Günter, Köln: Die USA auf dem Weg in eine multiethnische Gesellschaft: Ergebnisse des Zensus 2010. In: Geographische Rundschau 63 (2), 2011, S. 64 83. |Picture-Alliance GmbH, Frankfurt/M.: AP Images/Kurihara, Reiri 87; dpa 70; dpa/Levitt, Helen 123. |Shutterstock.com, New York: Balazik, Robert F. 91; Tatjana Russita 132. |stock.adobe.com, Dublin: Destina 68; pixmatu 62. |Süddeutsche Zeitung - Photo, München: Melde Press 95. |Wrong Hands / John Atkinson, Ottawa ON: "Vintage Social Networking" by John Atkinson (By granting the use of the cartoon titled "Vintage Social Networking" for one-time publication use in this textbook, I (John Atkinson) am in no way relinquishing the copyright, reproduction rights or intellectual property on this cartoon or on any other cartoon/artwork on the Wrong Hands site.) 120.